God's Turntable

by Shirley Wride

Published by Shirley Wride

Prepared for publication by
MediaHubAsia
Hong Kong • Bangkok

ISBN 978-0-9571556-0-2

Distributed by Bay Foreign Language Books Ltd.
Unit 4, Kingsmead, Park Farm, Folkestone, Kent.
CT19 5EU. England
Tel. +44 (0)1233 720123 Fax. +44 (0)1233 721272
www.baylanguagebooks.co.uk sales@baylanguagebooks.co.uk

AUTHOR'S ACKNOWLEDGEMENT
My sincere thanks to my nephews, Geoffrey and Nigel Lilburn, for their continuous help and patience in getting this manuscript ready for publication; also to my friend David Muirhead who proofread the final manuscript with me. My thanks also to St Swithun's School for permission to use the photo on Page 31

NOTE
Some real-life names have been changed to extend privacy to individuals

Preface

This book is quite simply the story of my life. There are no embellishments but, for personal reasons, there are some omissions. I started writing my diary in the 1950s after the Lord clearly told me: 'write down all of my dealings with you.' Some things were only jotted down in note form, others in great detail so as not to forget the impact they had on me at the time.

Shirley: 2010

For some years now I have known this book should be written. Twice I tried, getting so far but no further; I could neither find a good title, nor how I should write it. Then in 1986, I knew I had to try again. So this time I prayed to be given the title and how I should set about it. The title, *God's Turntable*, came very clearly to me during one of my quiet times. Also I knew it was to be an autobiography so I started right from the beginning. Now the writing flowed from my mind, I knew what to include and what not to. None of the previous difficulties occurred.

This, then, is the story of God's life in and through mine, not the other way round. It is the struggle of saying 'Thy will Lord' not 'Mine be done.' Without Him, this could never have happened as I would have chosen something very different. To Him, therefore, must go all the praise and glory as He alone has brought it to pass and, in consequence, must be the author of it.

Shirley Wride
Hythe, Kent

Chapter 1

“It’s a girl Mr Wride.’ Three times my father had hoped for a son, no doubt to follow in his footsteps as a pharmacist. But, alas, three times my mother had produced only girls. Now number four had arrived. As most women had their babies at home in those days (1928), our family doctor plus hired nurse were present for the great arrival. I arrived into this lovely world in the early hours of 23 July. The story goes that when the doctor went downstairs to inform my father of the new arrival and what sex it was, Daddy went immediately upstairs into the delivery room saying: ‘Four ruddy girls!’ But there was nothing to be done about it, there I was and there I intended to stay. I weighed eight pounds something and had rosy cheeks just like my dad. Actually, I don’t think Daddy was really bothered by the sex; it was just that he would have liked to have had a son. Anyway as years later proved me dead from the neck upwards at maths, a fine pharmacist I would have made.

Shirley: earliest surviving photo

Only a few memories remain of our first home (at 74 Hatherley Road, Winchester, Hants) where I was born; some were mere incidents, others were precious beyond words.

Most things were delivered in those days. Mr Coffin the baker (his name was written on his cart) came with his horse and cart. He selected bread from inside the double doors at the back, placing them in a lovely crispy, crackly basket. Hanging the basket over his arm, he opened our front gate and came to the door. Hearing the bell, Mummy and I would go and open it. Oh the heavenly smell that issued from the basket as Mummy chose the loaves. The Cobourg loaf with its four crusty corners, or maybe it was a tin loaf which was wanted for sandwiches for a picnic we were planning in the country. Then there was the cottage loaf, with one circle of bread sitting on a larger one, so tempting to tear off in order to scoop out the soft fluffy piece below. But things like that weren't done, it would have been considered naughty. With the exchange of money and a polite 'Good morning Madam,' the baker retraced his steps, closing our gate behind him. With a hop, skip and a jump he was on the footplate with the reins in his hands, then off would go baker, horse, cart and all.

1933: Shirley at Hatherley Road

The milkman also came along the same route and he had an amazing horse, far cleverer than the baker's. This horse knew instinctively when and where to go, and where and when to stop. It never occurred to me at that tender age that the poor animal had done the rounds so often it could have done them in its sleep. The cart also intrigued me. Firstly, it had only two wheels instead of the baker's four and, when the milkman stepped onto the rear step, it almost reached the ground. Great big milk churns stood in the back of the cart. Mummy would go to the door and, while I held the jug, the milk was carefully ladled into it. I would say that the milk was creamier than it is today. I'm sure the milkman never dreamed of big words like 'pasteurised, homogenised, skimmed, long life, gold topped,' to complicate his rounds. Milk was milk, straight from the cow into the churn, certainly straight from the churn into our jug. When the required amount had been ladled in, the milkman took his leave, carefully closing our gate behind him. His horse, needless to say, had already walked on to the next port of call.

One little episode still stands out clearly in my mind. I didn't feel very well one day after dinner so I curled up in a big armchair with a cover over me and fell asleep. When I eventually awoke I was amazed to see the table had been cleared of dinner things, the cloth folded up and put away, and the vase of flowers was back in the centre of the table. Everything had been silently stacked onto the three-tier trolley father had made; it had been wheeled into the kitchen and I hadn't heard a sound. To this day I shall never understand how it was done without my hearing. But such is the sleep of children.

I shared a bedroom with sister number three (Audrey); in it stood the BBC, the Big Brown Cupboard. All our personal treasures were kept in it; toys, games, dressing up clothes, books, it was treasure trove. Occasionally we had to tidy it up but we didn't do that very often; the items were pulled out, and then stuffed back into the cupboard when finished with. Dolls held little interest for me although they were beautifully outfitted by Mummy's nimble fingers and her excellent knitting and sewing skills.

I remember our celluloid dolls whose eyes closed when laid down. Each of us had a cot and pram for them, again outfitted my Mummy, and given as either birthday or Christmas presents. But they never did for me what I think they did for most children. I wasn't thrilled when bathing them or putting them to bed, and seldom hugged or nursed them. But just give me an animal! Oh how I adored them and still do. Three of my 'specials' remain vividly in my mind.

Dolls? No great interest for Shirley despite their outfits. With sister Audrey

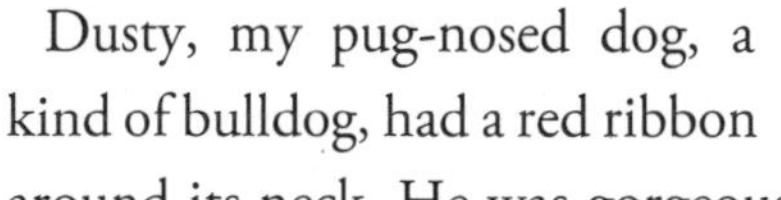

Dusty, my pug-nosed dog, a kind of bulldog, had a red ribbon around its neck. He was gorgeous, soft to the touch, and very obedient. He was stuffed with straw, and stood firmly on four legs. We were great pals. Larry, my white lamb, was of a gentler disposition and would occasionally collapse if I left her standing too long. I think the stuffing in one of her legs was thin, and the lower part of her leg crumpled beneath her. Poor darling, I always gave great consideration in this matter, and never let her stand for too long at a time. She was woollier than Dusty was and wore a pink ribbon around her neck. She stood just as firmly as I did, that is, until her leg let her down.

But my favourite, my own beloved, my more precious and most admired was Pinkie, my other dog. Sadly, Pinkie was no longer young. Like many an older person he had grown not only very thin on top but everywhere else; almost hairless. He sat on his haunches, front legs upright, as if waiting for a command from me, or a bone or something. His long ears hung down devoid of fur. Secretly, I admitted, he resembled the colour of a pig. Oh, my poor Pinkie! But he was beautiful in my eyes. I adored him. Talking of eyes, the feature I loved most about him was that his eyes were on wires and had become loose. They could be taken out. Oh the fun I had, pulling them out by degrees, watching the ever changing expression on his face. His patience was super-human. Never did he complain or take offence, even when I laughed at him. Folk speak of people's eyes standing out on stalks but I had a dog whose eyes stood out on wires. Much more fun or so I thought. Slowly I would pull the eyes out, one at a time, examine them closely, and then plunge them back into the same holes again. It's a wonder I didn't try to swallow them as I did the contents of peppermint toothpaste, still my favourite flavour, or when I ate some of Mummy's cold cream. Of course nowadays, eyes like that would be considered dangerous to children which they were but, worse still, I would probably have been sent to a psychiatrist and examined as to the reason for those sadistic tendencies at such a tender age, especially seeing I expressed such outward devotion and love for my pet dog. Happily, psychiatrist or no psychiatrist, such tendencies soon faded and only intense love for all kinds of animals remains. I remember neither the arrival nor departure of darling Pinkie. Perhaps with the passage of time he just fell apart at the seams or just faded out of my life. His final resting place remains a mystery.

Early 'sadistic' tendancies

Shirley and pet dog with parents, and sisters from left: Monica, Audrey and Barbara (with glasses)

Christmases were always a great source of preparation and excitement. Among my father's many gifts was photography. He was a member of the Photographic Society in Winchester, filming many of the events that took place there during his lifetime. As a reward for his services, he was given a copy of each film he took (and donated to the society). Maybe my memory is better for seeing our own amateur theatricals on film, but most of the events are clearly imprinted on my mind. Christmas never started as early as it does these days. Christmas cards in the shops in August was absolutely unheard of in the 1930s. Admittedly Mummy made the puddings well in advance which, when cooked, sat on the very top of our old-fashioned dresser with their heads tied up in a white cloth. Each year the same silver treasures (old silver sixpences) were hidden deep inside the pudding. I suppose the previous finders licked them clean, leaving them on the sides of their plates to be recollected and I trust sterilised before their next entry into the dark depths of the newly-made puddings. All of us helped make the cake and no doubt the puddings. Ingredients were weighed out, fruit washed, candy peeled, cut up and glacé cherries chopped or sliced. Almonds were soaked in hot, or was it boiling, water to remove their skins. How I loved squeezing them until they exploded out of their skins. Oh Lord, not another reminiscence of my sadistic tendencies? When everything was ready, the ingredients were put into a large mixing bowl and mixed by hand. We had no electric food mixers in those days and no fridge. Also things didn't come in ready mixed packets; so we started from scratch every time. I remember stirring the mixture together but it was heavy going with such a small hand on such a large wooden spoon. Finally, when everything was as Mummy thought it should be, the mixture was put into a well-greased cake tin and wrapped around with brown paper so that it wouldn't burn on the outside before it was cooked on the inside. It was then carefully placed into our blue New World cooker and left to cook slowly for hours and hours. The smell of that heated paper nearly made me sick and, by the time that cake was cooked, the whole house was permeated with it. Nearer the day we helped make marzipan and iced the outside of the cake, placing pretty objects on the smooth white surface. Finally a frilly frill finished the decorations to perfection. The cake was then placed in the larder.

We also made our own paper chains out of strips of coloured paper. There may have been some glue on the end of each strip which we wetted to form the rings. Otherwise flour and water made a good paste. We linked the rings together to form long chains. It was such a simple pleasure that brought much enjoyment. Of course, there was no television to amuse us; we had to make our own amusements. We may have started to decorate the Christmas tree but most of this was done after we had gone to bed on Christmas Eve; certainly not weeks ahead.

The first time I was taken into Winchester to see the Christmas lights was a great thrill. I don't think we ever shopped except in the mornings so to be taken in the afternoon when it was already getting dark was a great treat, especially when it was linked with the growing excitement of Christmas. The shops seemed so romantic in the artificial light with the street lights on.

By the time Christmas Eve arrived, we were all wild with excitement. On going to bed, we hung stockings at the bottom of our beds on the rails or posts. I never did catch Father Christmas putting presents in. Eventually we fell asleep only to wake up early on Christmas Day, crawling to the bottom of our beds and reaching down to the stockings which were oozing with presents and goodies. We then scrambled back into bed with them and started the thrill of discovering what Father Christmas had left us. We knew this invisible hand as Santa Claus. Slowly we pulled out the gifts, reasonably quietly I might add, in case Mummy and Daddy were still asleep. There was always a toy sticking out of the top of our stockings.

I especially remember little tins of biscuits of all shapes and sizes. How I loved them and it is highly possible that most of them were eaten there and then in bed.

But, as the household awoke, how many times I wonder did we have to refill our stockings so that the photographer (my father) might film the event? With a constant stream of instructions we did as we were told, the camera focused on first one then another and on one bed and then the other. The first session of filming over for the day, we leapt out of bed, washed and dressed, and raced downstairs to admire the newly decorated house. There were large and small paper bells of lovely colours plus paper chains of different designs and colours attached to the central light reaching into the four corners of the room. Balloons, holly, mistletoe and piles of presents we hoped were in the drawing room, all beautifully wrapped and tied up. And look, there are the paper chains we made; 'don't they look lovely!' The drawing room was out of bounds until after breakfast I recall; surprise, surprise. What did those Christmas breakfasts consist of? Cold ham, sausages, toast, marmalade, and tea? At last the great moment we had been waiting so long for had arrived. The fire was already alight so the room was nice and warm. It looked so lovely. But where are my presents? Ah, over there, I see them in that chair in the corner. Are all those presents for me? With a mad rush, we whipped off the lovely wrapping paper to see what was inside. Paper, string, tags, ribbon, the lot was strewn all over the floor. Was the gift of music already apparent in me when I received a large humming top? I would work it up to frenzy, and then become lost in the magical sound it produced as it spun round and round on the floor, ablaze with diffused colours. Why did it have to end?

Christmas dinners were traditional; turkey or chicken with all the trimmings, roast potatoes and sprouts picked from the garden. Mummy's two sisters known as the aunts (May and Connie), her brother and his son (Uncle Eddie and Ron) usually joined the happy throng each year. I suppose the aunts helped with the preparations, perhaps we had a maid at that time but I'm not sure but I never remember helping with the work in the kitchen. Mummy decorated the dinner table beautifully. When the feast was ready, we all gathered round the table in the dining room, crackers with horrible bangs and more horrible hats were pulled, then Daddy started carving the bird. We passed our plates up the table for a serving and vegetables and helped ourselves to the etceteras. We always received a helping of that delicious accompaniment called stuffing. I think it made the meal.

With the first course eaten, the table was cleared for a ceremonial arriving of the pudding. Curtains were drawn and the magic spirit poured over it, somebody struck a match and the pudding was set alight. In the semi-darkness we watched it begin to burn amid the 'Oooos' and the 'Arhhhs' from the aunts who raised their arms upwards, palms towards the pudding which was now enveloped in a blue flame as if they were seeing an apparition. When our eyes had readjusted to the light again, the pudding was sliced and a portion was given to each person. How I hated eating it and Christmas cake for that matter. It was so sickly but I had to eat a tiny bit as none of us was allowed to become 'faddy.' Now I'm grown up I try not to touch either although eating it does not have the same nauseating effect any more. But I still don't like the taste. Anyway, Mummy made it tolerable by making sure that I got one of the silver objects which had been re-hidden from the previous years. There were also jam tarts and mince pies, the latter also having the same nauseating effect on me. To end the feast, absent friends were toasted and thought of, silly hats discarded, and all hands made light work of removing the remnants that were stacked onto the three-tier trolley and wheeled away to the kitchen. Tradition in our family left the washing up to the male species. What a comedown for them, I always thought.

I expect we children played with all our new toys and things after lunch while the older folk struggled with their falling eyelids, finally coming to when a cup of tea appeared later on. How anyone could stuff a piece of cake inside at tea time was quite beyond my understanding but some did. Finally I never remember having to eat a piece of Christmas cake, only the pudding.

Later we played games together which included the grown-ups. The photographer was always around with his instructions, recording incidents that would keep alive our memories until the end of our days (as long as the celluloid survived). As discussions, games or whatever came to an end and our bedtime fast approached, the mystery masterpiece that ended all our Christmases was about to have its yearly airing; Auld Lang Sine. Mummy, a most accomplished pianist, seated herself at the pianoforte. Daddy stood poised as ever with his cine camera plus the usual string of instructions that always seemed to him so necessary to put us on film. While the rest of us made a large circle around the room, Mummy struck up the first chords loud and clear. We all crossed arms, holding hands with our neighbours (relations in our case) to form a continuous chain. Singing 'should auld acquaintance be forgot' started the chain rotating in one direction, and the photographer's instructions. Round and round the room we went to the rhythm of the music; sopranos, altos, tenors, and bases trying to keep pitch on overblown stomachs; not easily done, while the chain of arms began to rise and fall beating chests and breasts alike. Faster and faster, louder and louder went the human chain. On the very audible instructions from the film producer (it was a silent movie), the chain suddenly changed direction. In and out it went, one moment I was almost squeezed to death on the inside only to be stretched apart on the outside. It was torture being so small. Then with the final crescendo rising to fortissimo on the piano and sopranos, altos, tenors and bases blasting beyond belief we reached the grand finale. What singing, what did it all mean? I never knew then and I still don't; tradition?

So the performance was over for yet another year and with stomachs bursting to capacity the ghastly round of kissing relations goodnight began. Uncle (Eddie) always kissed me on my lips which I dreaded and hated. It made me feel sick. I can't say that I have changed much in this respect either over the years. So the final instructions from the film producer two very tired but happy little girls could be seen forever on film going slowly up the stairs to bed in their dressing gowns and slippers. What a lovely day it had been and what lovely memories to cherish throughout the passing years.

The aunts (May and Connie) and uncle (Eddie) had a house in

Southampton. At some period in their lives Auntie May, I think it was, bought a dear little house in the country, halfway between Southampton and Winchester at Otterbourne. Every evening during the war, they hastily drove out of Southampton in the evening and slept at this little house to avoid the night bombing. It was while they were there that they lost their (Southampton) property in a night raid. They salvaged what they could and made the little house their permanent home.

Going to the aunts for tea was a

Above: 'The aunts.' From left: May, Shirley's mother (Getrude Wride, neé Clark), and Connie

Right: The 'dear little house' bought by the aunts, Norman Meade, at Otterbourne, Hants. Photo taken by Shirley in 1968

great treat. The house stood well off the main road and all was peace and quiet. A huge oak tree grew to the right of the driveway and a circular flower bed was thick with yellow crocuses in the spring. A Virginia creeper had crept over the front walls of the house. From the upstairs windows there was a wonderful view of the countryside. In autumn, the creeper turned to a marvellous crimson. I felt one step back in time at the aunts; actually I looked upon them with a bit of awe at that age. They were so proper and we had to behave proper too, not that we were ever allowed to do anything else, but somehow it had to be real proper when visiting these dear maiden ladies. After the greetings on arrival had been made under the arched porch where the clematis climbed and rambled at leisure, we were ushered into a tiny hall and helped off with coats which were then hung on the hall stand. It had two troughs where umbrellas and walking sticks were kept. Gloves, if any, were laid on top of the glove box and a quick glance in the small central mirror, a wee bit high for me, soon told me if our coiffeur was as it should be. We were then led into the front room. The room was jammed with furniture, far too large and heavy-looking for such a small a room. Big pictures looked heavily down on us from the walls and I had a feeling of being enclosed in a box, especially as the room was in tones of brown.

Those aunts, and uncle (Eddie) and his son (Ron) were great gardeners and a tour of the garden was inevitable. Donning their hats, even on a summer's day, the aunts led the way through the back door into the garden. There was a long concrete path running the whole length of the garden which always made me feel that the house had its tongue poking out. Patches of grass and a lattice led to the fruit and vegetable garden. I remember seeing weeds but never mentioned it; it would not have been proper. We followed reverently behind our elders trying to feel grown up, commenting, admiring but mostly just listening to all we were shown. The plum tree has never been so good as this year, said the aunt. Just look at the branches laden with fruit. The fruit branches had been propped up on poles so the beautiful purple plums, still with their blooms, wouldn't break. Indeed it was a wonderful year for fruit - and wasps for that matter. Here and there, hanging at random, jam jars with jam at the bottom swung with their ghastly contents; crawling through the holes in the paper lids, the jam jars were seething with a mass of dead, dying or soon would-be newly caught wasps. A more revolting sight you couldn't imagine. There were espalier apples, red and black currant bushes covered with old net curtains to keep the birds off, gooseberry bushes, marrows growing on mounds of compost wandering like snakes in the long grass. Each marrow, whether yellow or green striped, had a neat piece of wood under it to keep the slugs away and the marrows clean.

Vegetables were always excellent as the soil was so good, enriched with their own compost. By the garden gate at the end of the concrete path, which led into a large field, we peeped into a tiny greenhouse full of seeds and plants. One of the aunts had bought the field to avoid it being built on. I believe that when she eventually sold it years later she received as much for each plot, three in all, as she had originally paid for the entire field. How I loved that field. The grasses and wild flowers grew almost as high as I was. A laburnum tree blossomed in spring with a golden mass of hanging chains. In autumn, I remember a crab apple tree laden with pom-poms, and searching for the odd mushroom kept us quiet many an afternoon. Bees 'zeeed' in the flowers and the tiny blue and brown butterflies flitted about the flower faces. Birds sang and always the cuckoo could be heard in the distant woods from April onwards. There was a summer house at the top of the field; it was wonderful just sitting up there looking over the distant hills.

Sometimes we had afternoon tea there as well but it was a very long way to carry it all from the house. Many times we walked along the lane; it was so peaceful with few houses and fewer cars. Primroses, bluebells and anemones grew in profusion under the hazelnut bushes whose catkins dripped pollen on everything. Later in the year, scabious, red campion, ragwort, marguerites and dandelions painted the fields and hedgerows with colour. In the autumn, long strands of wild bryony would shine with berries and twine themselves among the red hips of the wild roses. Sometimes we found a pin cushion among them. There were spindle trees with bunches of vivid pink lanterns hanging down, some having burst open showing their tiny orange berry seeds inside waiting to leap out of the cases.

Today, however, was blackberrying day. Clad in our old clothes we turned off the lane and clambered over the style, walking through a field of cows that looked at us with their big tragic eyes and long eyelashes. They only looked at us, thank goodness, as we passed, us trudging on further where the berries glistened between the wicked thorns that protected them we started to pick. At first I ate more than I put in the punnet. The pips got stuck between my uneven teeth which needed a long fingernail, a thing I never seemed to have, to extricate them. Already my fingers and tongue had turned a magnificent purple from the berries that had been squashed between them, specks of blood brought to the surface from the thorns were licked off as they appeared on my fingers. Scratches were ignored; who cared anyway? It was a wonderful world; peace, beauty, birdsong and great fun.

Back at the house we awaited tea, prepared as always with loving care. Thinly cut bread and butter, at least two kinds of home-made jam, home-made cakes on glass stands or a silver cake dish always with a pretty doily underneath. All this was set on a white hand-worked tablecloth with dainty floral china on a large table in the small dining room. Each jam had its own spoon and even the butter, if it came onto the table, had a funny shaped knife all to itself. There were spoons set for fruit but we never knew what it would be until we had had our fill – well almost – of bread and butter and cakes.

The aunts, having now excused themselves from the table could be heard with a tin opener in the kitchen. Slowly the curtain which hung on the inside of the dining-room door against draughts would rise a little from the carpet as both the ladies came back, one with a bowl of fruit, the other with a jug of cream. We never dared ask what kind of fruit we were going to have as that would not have been proper. As both aunts were capable of saying 'and what makes you think you're going to have fruit?' So we sat and waited for the surprise. Sitting bolt upright in the high backed chair, my legs dangling, we continued our tea with the long heavily-framed pictures watching us from the walls and their heavy net curtain over the window keeping out most of the light.

The chimes of the clock striking every quarter completed the scene and the atmosphere. Every time we visited my aunts I felt the same feeling of awe as if I had stepped back into a bygone age. They have all gone now, and so has the peace of that lovely country lane. Where the watercress beds were there are now houses, the lane is wider and straighter connecting two main roads. Heavy traffic thunders past. The little house, Norman Meade, is still there but just down the lane and over the field where we picked the blackberries you can see and, alas, hear the incessant roar of traffic from the flyover connecting Winchester to Southampton.

I wonder if the cuckoo goes there nowadays. I don't want to visit there again; the memories of my childhood must remain as they were or else they won't be treasured any more.

One of the first of many precious moments in my life took place in our first home where I was born. These moments began very early in my life. In fact I've never known a time when they didn't exist. Our garden was large and long on three levels, each level led down to the next by a series of steps. Both my parents were great gardeners, tending with loving care all the flowers and vegetables alike. How glad I am to have inherited this gift of being able to lose myself in the peace and tranquillity that gardening brings. The prized peony grew in the corner by the first flight of steps leading down to the second level. My sister (Audrey) and I used to jump over it onto the grass below; it was a risky business as we would have been severely reprimanded had we damaged the beautiful plant. A neat square lawn surrounded by flowers with a lattice on which roses grew and a gravel path leading to the third level comprised the second section. Down the next flight of steps was the largest and the longest area. Vegetables plus flowers were grown here and at the bottom stood a summer house. To the right of the steps was my joy, a beautiful rockery. Here was the very first of my heavenly hideouts. In spring it was a riot of colour; yellow and white alyssum, purple aubretia, white cerastium, anemonies, commonly called wind flowers (can you think of anything more exquisite in concept than a flower born on the wind?), daffodils, grape hyacinths, tulips and no doubt many more that I can't recall.

When it was ablaze with colour it came alive with the music of humming bees flitting from one flower to another. The flowers, as if doing obeisance on their hosts, bowed their heads under the weight of their almost weightless guests who were now covered with golden pollen. After the guests departed, the flowers would shyly raise their heads again. Here was heaven itself come down to earth. I was filled with a wonder and a beauty I did not understand. As I sat on the path and beheld this beauty of colour and sound, I became a part of what I was seeing and hearing. I was on an eye level with it and somehow felt inside it or it was inside of me, a kind of spiritual presence was experienced. This presence was always with me but became intensified during times like this. No words could express it. I don't think I meditated, because I doubt whether I knew what it meant at that age but I definitely experienced some form of inner glory which I never wanted to lose. It enveloped me in that aloneness.

The thought of a picnic was always a great thrill as we went into the country. It all started the day before with the preparation of making sandwiches known as 'the eats.' We children helped by spreading the bread with butter. After buttering each slice they were laid side-by-side so they would match perfectly when put together. Eggs were hard-boiled, cucumber and tomato sliced and placed neatly on the bread adding salt or vinegar, I forget which. And then on went the lids, perhaps we had sardine and meat sandwiches as well but whatever it was the saliva in my mouth ran at the thought of eating them the next day. Sometimes little bits of filling fell out and were greedily devoured by the first hand that could grab and pick them up. I was already in the country with the birds and the bees and the beautiful sound of the wind in the trees. Finally all hands were needed to hold the piles of various sandwiches together in order that the bread saw could cut through diagonally without them falling to pieces. Each pile was then wrapped in greaseproof paper and marked so we would know which was which when we opened them again. They were tenderly stacked together and placed in a very large light blue bread bin that was housed on the brick floor in the larder (no fridge). Next day the big black picnic box was brought down from its hiding place and filled with 'the eats' and the drinks.

Just before we set off, it was strapped to the back of the car, with rugs, tarpaulin, everything except the kitchen sink, and we set off. We four girls dare not make trouble at the back as Daddy got so irritated with our noise. If we wanted to argue it had to be done in utter secrecy. Finally when we arrived at the spot our parents had decided upon we came to a halt. Now there were birds to observe through binoculars, songs to recognise, botany lessons on the wild flowers, butterflies to watch and identify plus the usual instructions from the photographer who as usual wanted it all on film.

A rabbit takes a long hard look at us as we invade his plot, picking wild strawberries, and then making a dash to safety. Butterflies flit from place to place, yes we knew their names already and most of the wild flowers as well. We listened attentively to the birdsong to make sure we had the right song for the right bird. We ran, jumped, skipped, watched and listened. The silence was heaven, deepened by some distant murmur of running water, rustling of leaves, or twittering of birds; only the occasional shouts from us broke the exquisite solitude and quietness, a quietness where one could grow inwardly. On one such picnic, I raced after my three sisters and fell on a large stone. My left knee was badly cut. Daddy washed it with water and bound it declaring that it would have to be stitched. I was filled with fear at the thought. It never was stitched and to this day I have a wide scar to show for it.

But at last came the moment I had been waiting for; it was time for the 'eats.' The tarpaulin and rugs were spread out and the picnic box unstrapped from the car. Plates, knives, forks, spoons, serviettes etc were laid out, flasks of water for tea, milk, sugar and possibly fruit juices for us. Finally the sandwiches made their appearance; each packet was unfolded and left just as it was. Which pile was the cucumber? Where are the tomato ones? Where have the ham ones gone? Oh don't say we left the hard-boiled eggs behind? No, there they are hiding behind those serviettes. I couldn't eat fast enough, I swallowed great unchewed lumps and felt them agonisingly descend, and then I had to wait until each lump made its painful way lower and lower. Oh boy did it hurt. But it was worth it every time. I stuffed until I couldn't eat another morsel. Oh such wonderful 'eats.'

Soon we were off again exploring among the trees and bushes, scuffling through crackly twigs and dead leaves. There was no danger in those days; we wandered about with no fear at all. Alas it was all too soon time to pack up and return home, so we left the birds to go to bed and the flowers to close their petals and whatever night creature wanted to wake up to its own little world while we returned to our known little world. Those magical moments remain deeply impressed in my mind.

Chapter 2

Beaconsfield House and conservatory in the 1930s

When I was eight years old we moved into our next house on the outskirts of Winchester. My only recollection was that every time we went there beforehand Mummy produced watercress sandwiches for tea which we ate in the conservatory. What a lovely taste those sandwiches had and with such a delectable smell. The house stood on a corner on its own ground off Andover Road. There was a long drive leading to the south side and off to the left were the stables, harness room and coach house. Having no horses, we stored wood and coal in the stables, cutting up all the wood between us for the fires with a two handled saw. The harness room housed bicycles and a large mangle plus general odds and ends. Between these two was the coach house but, like Cinderella, the hour of midnight had struck and both she and the coach had gone so Daddy kept his car in it. Above these three places was the hayloft where we kept all sorts of things, dare I say junk?

At times we danced to a gramophone and always stored the apples there after they had been harvested from the garden. How well I remember the cold winter of 1947; one of our pipes burst spewing water which

Beaky and grounds taken in the mid-80s. Stables and coach house still on left

had frozen into a cascade of ice. It looked so lovely; the trees had their branches encased in ice and what a fantastic sound it was to hear the clicking and clacking as they blew against each other in the wind. We had stored the apples as usual in the hayloft and knew what would happen to them directly the thaw set in. When it did they turned rotten almost overnight. We collected the brown squashy apples in great galvanised baths, and dumped them in the copse at the side of the driveway. There was a smell of cider for quite some time. In this copse stood my favourite trees, tall and stately; I loved playing in there. We rigged up a swing on a large branch, swinging on it until the branch died and eventually broke off. We also climbed trees to watch the bank holiday traffic which had accumulated on Andover Road. We all had to pull our weight in the garden, hence our knowledge of it came quite naturally and, as Daddy insisted on the Latin names for everything, we learned them too. It was a huge garden comprising lawns, flower beds and pathways later to be edged with my father's rustic latticework on which rambler roses were trained. We grassed one huge area calling it the tennis court, and played on it quite often. I was never any good at tennis as my hands, being so small, couldn't grip the racket firmly enough. Consequently the racket just twisted in my hand when the ball hit it. I never liked games, anyway, except netball which I became quite good at.

The words 'Clean all Tools' were written in large letters on the whitewashed wall in the conservatory. All tools had their rightful place on nails and woe betide any of us if we did not firstly wash them clean in a water butt just inside the door with the brush provided, let alone not put them back in their place. Springtime brought out daffodils by the hundreds, crocuses, tulips and snowdrops, wallflowers and a host of other early flowers. Through the frozen ground, tiny shoots began to appear, at first only a speck and then the blades pushed their way up through the hard earth where neither fork nor trowel could penetrate. The snowdrops with their snow-white skirts, then crocuses leaning against the long blades of grass pushing them aside as the sun opened their cups of variegated colours. In the gravel park in front of the conservatory grew iris stylosa with their pale mauve flowers lasting only one day; patches of celandine glistened like butter between grey stones. All too soon the lawns had to be cut, digging, hoeing, weeding, preparing, planning, sowing, planting, watching and waiting. I loved it when we went out to buy the packets of seeds. I wanted to grow everything I saw. The laburnum tree came into bloom with its long yellow chains of separate flowers, the May tree with its free gift of perfume to all who passed. There was white and mauve lilac, philadelphus (mock orange) with its almost overpowering scent. Next the herbaceous plants came into their own, delphiniums, lupines, hollyhocks, madonna lilies with their long stamens marking the spotless petals with golden stain. A lavender hedge lined both sides of a narrow path needing only the brush of a leg to send the scent spiralling into the air. Later we gathered the purple heads of seeds in pretty muslin bags with bows around their necks, their destination would be draws, wardrobes, or just hanging around. Between two brambly apple trees, big red poppies bloomed among the long grass. Bees would zzzzzzz among the stamens emerging like fluffy balls of gold dust. Over on the dividing wall to the other house we grew gooseberries, loganberries, and a thornless blackberry. Also a buddleia attracted all sorts of butterflies. I recall dozens of them; red admirals, peacocks, tortoiseshells, painted ladies, commas (the comma butterfly has ragged outlines to their wings as if they have been torn; reddish brown in colour with darker spots; rare these days), cabbage whites and many more.

Mid 30s: Early love of nature

Autumn, my favourite of all the seasons, brought the rewards of our labours. We enjoyed the dahlias that crowded the flower beds with their bright open faces of every imaginable colour. Also chrysanthemums in pink, bronze, yellow, white and mauve, bringing one of the last splashes of colour before early winter set in. We harvested the potatoes, laying them out to dry, and then brushing off the earth before storing them in sacks. Carrots were dug and buried in huge boxes of sand. Parsnips were left until they had been frosted and then dug as needed. Tomatoes were stored in the loft to ripen. Most of the fruit had been picked and what had not been eaten, bottled or stored, was made into jam. I can see my mother to this day sitting on a high stool in the scullery, stirring the slowly cooking fruit with a large wooden spoon in one hand and holding a book in the other. She must have sat there for hours, constantly putting a little of the would-be jam on the edge of a saucer to see if it would gel.

Age 10: 'magic moments' in the garden

The lawns didn't need cutting so often because of the dew, and autumn slowly spread her beautiful colours through the trees, in the fields and the hedgerows. The hips and haws looked as though they had been polished for a special occasion. The Michaelmas daisies dotted about the garden with a few phlox still in bloom. I would wander among the low growing bushes, briony twined around the tiny berries decorating the long strands. I saw the golden brown beech trees, red maple and bright green lime seeds with wings waiting to spiral down in the wind, the sycamore with its keys that opened every secret door. Against the blue sky, I watched the leaves come sailing and floating through the air like magic carpets with magical destinations. The wind would blow, bending and bowing the branches. Then would be heard a rustle and a scurry and down would come hundreds of chattering leaves making their final journey to the earth. They also kept us busy by sweeping and raking them up. Feeling the wind in my face and a chill coming over my body, I drew my arms around me as I walked on fallen twigs that cracked under my feet. The last roses bloomed on the lattice, and the huge seed heads of the red poppies reminded me of summer days. The snowball tree had leaves edged with crimson and the yew wore pink berries like fairy cups only highly poisonous. The silver birch with its tiny golden leaves stood quivering and shivering in the cool breeze. I walked up the driveway examining the yellow and red holly berries. I thought of Christmas with decorations, presents, turkey and sprouts, picked from the garden and lovely open log fires.

I started piano lessons when I was eight years old. In fact we all (all four sisters) learned. Mummy, being a good pianist herself, thought it imperative that we studied. I loathed practising but a notebook was kept which Mummy had to sign before our next lesson proving that we had indeed done 10 minutes practice a day. Years later I practised for hours on end just for the sheer joy of it. But escaping into the garden to find my heavenly hideouts was far more to my liking than dull old piano practice. Each year our very gifted lady music teacher gave a concert using all the talents available from her pupils plus her own. There were part-songs, dancing, duets, solos, sketches plus anything else she had thought up.

One concert episode stands out in my mind as though it were yesterday. It was time for my piano solo; the piece was called The Bee and of the Clover (John Thompson). Seated at the piano, legs dangling down, I started playing very grandly. All went well until the last chord which I couldn't find. I can't remember if I did eventually find it but Daddy saved the day by starting to applaud. I suppose I gave up and slid off the piano stool.

A cutting had been kept dated 4 December 1937 read as follows. 'One of the tinies ended the concert by singing Brahms' lullaby... ' Our teacher had put a bed on the stage and when I finish singing I crawled into it, my voice had been discovered right from that time.

'Formidable' Grandma, 1938 photo

The reason we moved into this large house off Andover Road was because grandma (Margaret Heathcote Wride, nee Jeeves), Daddy's mother, had had an attempted burglary in her home and didn't feel safe living alone, hence we joined forces. The house (Beaconsfield House) was divided into two sections with two staircases, a door from the hall plus one on the landing above cut the house nicely into two halves. The final flight of stairs led up to the attic comprising one very large and one much smaller room. Grandma's companion occupied the smaller room. The other was our play room. Both rooms had dormer windows and low ceilings so very little light entered. A few more steps led up under the eves where a tiny window let out on to the flat part of the roof, out of bounds to us of course, although Daddy did some fire-watching from those dizzy heights during the war. Grandma had her sitting room off the hall, next to our dining and drawing room. One of her windows overlooked the driveway. The front stairs with her carpet was hers, for adults only. We were expected to use the other staircase known as the back stairs at all times.

Grandma was a formidable woman, large busted and with very little hair left on her head. She wore a hair piece with a black bow attached to it. Her back was like a ramrod and I think she had been one of 16 children. She referred to herself as the policeman of the family. As far as I was concerned she almost wrecked our family life; we children could do nothing right. She retired to bed quite early so we had to be absolutely quiet even though our sleeping quarters were at the back of the house. 'Don't wake mother!' If we heard Daddy say it once we heard it a hundred times. We were allowed to cycle around the garden on our bikes but directly Grandma knew we were doing this she would go out and lock the green gates that divided the back half of the garden from the garage and driveway. Not being allowed to ride in front of her sitting room window, there was no way we were able to get to the harness room to put our bikes away. There was a continual Cold War going on in our home. Did we dare to try and cycle in front of her sitting room without being caught? I seem to remember we did.

There was only one bathroom in the entire house so we all had our times for using it. One day, my sister and I were bathing our dolls in it when the door was flung open and in marched that horrible all woman called Grandma. She informed us that the door must be left open 'if that's all you're doing.' How I hated her. She marred every pleasure of ours and was so severe with her simple-minded companion. On Sundays she walked to her place of worship, veiled and with a walking stick. Another of our dares was dashing up her front stairs when nobody was about. Halfway up, the enormous landing window commanded a lovely view over the driveway and the copse. To beat the horrible old woman at her game was sheer delight to me. Anyway I liked the view from the window. Why shouldn't I use her beastly stairs and wear out her horrible stair carpet. It was worth the risk every time and I always got away with it. Grandma also had her own section of the garden. In it stood the only Cox's Orange Pippin apple tree and I never hesitated to help myself when

Swinging on the tree of forbidden fruit

the apples were ripe enough to eat. An enormous bird cherry tree, a prunus avium, claimed as hers, white like snow with blossom, stood in an area away from the house. Behind it you couldn't be seen from the house side. It was shady and in spring wonderful clumps of polyanthus grew in profusion and bloomed to perfection. What fun; I was alone there, a heavenly hideout, but I couldn't relax. I was on enemy territory; Grandma's territory. Gazing upwards I could see the brown branches with hundreds of tiny white flowers and pale green leaves against the blue sky. I watched the clouds roll by, heard the gentle wind and no one knew I was there. Yes it was within me again, this indescribable something that surged through my innermost being.

Opposite the north side of the house was a side road with a row of houses, beyond these lay farm fields. Sometimes I would slip away unnoticed and wander around the edges of these fields of ripening corn or barley. The wind waved the stalks to and fro like a mighty restless sea; back and forth the waves swept in the wind, changing into different patterns and shades as the shadows cast from the clouds passing the sun tore across the golden sea in a frantic frenzy to get to the other side. An intensified joy overtook me, this aloneness but not loneliness left me incapable of other thoughts. It was sheer bliss, a feast of sight and sound. No matter where I am, silence is something I seek every day. It's an essential ingredient, I must have it.

I was the last one left at home when Grandma was finally put into a home, so I moved my bedroom from the back of the house to the front. Even her stairway was mine now but I was considerably older by then. By the time I had chosen a nice lino and arranged the room with my knickknacks and personal touches it was transformed.

This room overlooked the front lawn with central flowerbeds and a row of beautiful green beeches that divided us from the school grounds beyond. In the silence of Sunday morning, I would plant my elbows squarely on the open window sill overlooking the lawn and beech trees. The air was like wine, undisturbed over the still slumbering city. The scent from the newly-cut lawn rose up to meet me, filling my nostrils with its magnificent perfume. I gazed at the threads of gossamer cobwebs with their myriad of reflecting diamonds not yet glistening in the un-risen sun. They hung from the twigs and branches like strings of pearly lights, swaying back and forth in the whisper of the wind, hanging from the glossy laurel leaves and attached by long strands, the wonder weaver rested in the centre of his bedecked house like a fretwork of lace with strands drooping under the weight of the pearly dew drops which the night had bestowed upon it. It was a masterpiece of woven wonder, now billowing out like the sail of a yacht caught in an undercurrent of breeze, now returning to its place after the whispering breeze had passed. Through the huge green beeches, shafts of pale lemon sunlight silently pushed their beams on the now glistening lawn weaving an ever-changing pattern, now lengthening, now shortening. As a rising wind swayed the branches of the huge trees, they shimmered and shook; greeting and caressing each other in unspoken whispers of the newborn day. What secrets they had between themselves for no one else to hear.

1938: Shirley and sister Audrey (standing) at 'Beaky'

Down in the valley, Winchester Cathedral's bells began to herald the day. The sound gently lifted over the city, floated over the smoking chimneys, and wended its way through the sleeping gardens by the river. On and up it rose like music of another world. It swept through the fields and hedgerows, crept up the shafts of sunlight enveloping the pink fleecy clouds, flooding the entire valley with pure joy. It reached me as I leaned on the windowsill transporting me in spirit on wings of the morning into the great building itself. I stood among the ancient pillars that had stood over the centuries, holding up the magnificent vaulted gothic roof. I saw the flags, now faded and threadbare with time, the reredos with its wonderfully carved figures hanging like a lace curtain behind the coloured cloth on the alter. The candles winked and spluttered in an invisible breeze, dribbling melted wax that clung like beads to their sides. I walked over the stone floor, made uneven in places by the countless feet of generations. When the first notes of the organ shook the rafters, they thundered through the chapel isles enveloping the stone pillars and archways, passing through the wrought iron gates and up the steps to the choir; filling the carved choir stalls and pulpit they rose through the roof to the belfry. For a moment the sound fought for recognition with the peeling bells but as the first line of the hymn was taken up by the processing choir and the jewelled cross lifted high wended its way up the central aisle, each bell swung slower and lower into its place until the final tones were absorbed in the hills and trees and the valley returned to its silence once more.

What was this glory I experienced, this wonder, this sensation? Was it a form of worship; if so, for what? As long as I can remember this has always been a part of my life. It's so easy for me to slip into a world of wonderment and imagination where I feel healed, restored, perfected. It's on a higher plane altogether. The older I grew the more I experienced it but only in solitude was I enveloped by it. I felt free to dance with the clouds, race with the shadows, leap with the lambs, taste the dew drops and caress the wind. I could fly like a bird, sing like a nightingale, tumble with the thunder and dash through the lightning; oh it was a glorious wonderland that no-one else could enter. I was alone yet not alone. To delve unhindered into unknown depths, soar like an eagle on the wind into limitless space, into a timeless eternity.

Only recently I read these words by Oswald Chambers who wrote: 'Nature to a saint is sacramental. If we are children of God, we have a tremendous treasure in nature. In every wind that blows, in every night and day of the year, in every sign of the sky, in every blossoming and in every withering of the Earth there is a real coming of God to us if we will simply use our starved imagination to realise it.'

I think this gives me an answer to what I tried to explain and experienced in those days but could never understand.

By now, school was the order of the day. I hated every minute of it. The truth was I was terrified. Being so small I was teased by the bigger girls which embarrassed me. Not in a hundred years could I do any form of arithmetic, even today subtraction is fraught with problems. I was also very slow to learn, remaining bottom of the form throughout my entire school life. I'm sure I moved up only because I was too old to stay down. I was very good at art, music and letter-writing but those subjects didn't count for much then. My great problem was that I used to dream during lessons and it was only when I switched on again as it were did I realise that I had switched off at some time or other; a most unfortunate state of affairs. The comment on the end of term report usually said: 'Shirley could do better if she tried.' Well Shirley decided she would try to do better and made a stupendous effort one term but to no avail. It made not the slightest difference so she gave up. If you hate something and you are frightened of it, how can you be a success?

St Swithun's in 1945 *Photo kind permission of the school*

Our school, St Swithun's, was set on a hill and the wind howled through the north facing windows, playing music like an Aeolian harp. It was a wonderful sound. I spent quite a bit of time standing outside my classroom door for some reason or another listening to this wonderful music. Sometimes we went for nature study walks on the Downs. One day I was alone with my teacher collecting wild flowers when it started to rain. We sheltered in a milkman's van. I can still hear the rain beating down on the metal roof and the smell of sweat from our bodies. But the windows steamed up while the thunder roared and the lightning flashed. It was a thrilling moment.

I always gained high marks for flower identification; we had Daddy and Mummy to thank for that when we went on walks, rambles or picnics. Learning the names of flowers and grasses was all part of it. I inherited their love of nature, in fact we all did. I might not have been second from bottom in a class if we'd had television in those days as I retain things better if I can see them in pictures. Who knows?

Just one more memory concerning school and I won't mention the horrible subject again. The tailor who made our tunics told my mother I would be tall as I had very broad shoulders but alas I went through school wearing a gigantic hem that waited and waited to be let down but never seem to be, not fully anyway.

Growing up wasn't made easier by the war; there were different stresses, and different temptations right at one's doorstep. I was 11 when the war broke out but didn't grasp what it meant. All curtains had to be lined with blackout material. Daddy built a wooden frame with wire mesh over it which was slotted into place every evening over a large window at the bottom of a sloping passage leading to the kitchen. He considered the top of the passage the safest place in our house in an air raid. How often we huddled there when the siren sounded. Listening to those awful doodlebugs going overhead, and then came the moment of waiting when the noise stopped before an explosion. Fortunately Winchester escaped it all but we were still near enough to Southampton when it was bombed and set on fire. Daddy reported one night when he came down from watching on the roof that the sky was glowing red from the fires.

An American bakery was set up in huge area the other side of the garden wall. Officers came over one day to ask Daddy if they could borrow our tools to level the ground as the bakery was to be housed under great marquees. From then on, the smell of baking bread and ground coffee wafted over the wall into our garden. Sometimes we were given bread and cake. The Americans gave dances in the city to which we were invited. I loathed ballroom dancing but loved the sumptuous food that went with it. We ate things we hadn't seen since rationing began. Later we had commandos billeted on us, and later still we let rooms to married

A star in the making? Shirley (above) playing a lead roll in the Gilbert and Sullivan operetta, Trial by Jury

In search of singing success (left): Photos taken in 1949 and 1950

couples. People came round to look at the house and then told us how many people we were expected to put up. I never realised how much cooking Mummy must have done with the three commandos billeted on us. Like so much when one is younger, it is all taken for granted. We took sandwiches to school for lunch but every evening when we came home there was a lovely hot meal being kept for us. I never gave a thought to the hours of work involved.

Now and then we were given pieces of parachute from which we made slips and very good they were. Wool could be obtained with coupons but was nearly always cut so we didn't buy any. Once I did make a lovely jumper joining all the links together. Silly isn't it when you think about it.

One episode I remember very clearly but dared not report it. I used to take our dog out for walks on the Downs which was forbidden. I loved it up there; it was so peaceful and full of wild flowers. One day as I stood near a field I was surprised to see a light aircraft coming in to land on the opposite side. It landed and taxied straight towards me, coming to a halt close to where the dog and I were standing. Then, as if from nowhere, a man appeared with a package in his hand, handed it to the pilot with a few words, and then disappeared. The pilot lifted the tail of the plane, turned it round and took off in the direction from whence it had come. Just what did I witness that day? Perhaps nothing or perhaps something of great importance or secrecy, I shall never know.

Teenage years to my mind can never be easy, especially when you realise you are gifted with a good future before you. I was now very advanced with the piano, and had a coloratura voice well worth training, so my teacher pointed out. I dreamed of one thing only and that was of becoming a great singer. Mummy, being a musician herself, realised that to be a good singer, a good musical education was very necessary. Everything was certainly pointing in that direction, also the awareness that I was now growing attractive, and attracting the opposite sex, plus the longing to receive greater acclaim and applause made me become very conceited and I should imagine quite unbearable at times. I felt I was something. Joining the local operatic society, I took part in four performances of Gilbert and Sullivan's operas, taking leads in two of them. All this was inclined to send my pride and conceit even deeper; I was now somebody, limelight at last. With these glamorous self-centred thoughts, I slogged away at my piano lessons and my dreams with one aim in my mind; that nothing and no-one was going to stand in the way of my career.

We were brought up to go to church. Each Sunday we donned our Sunday best and either walked or went by car. I found making eyes to the choirboys far more interesting than the dull services. Had I been caught, my father would have been furious. He was a churchwarden, and on occasions read the lessons and would have been considered, as I heard some people say, a pillar of the church. This pillar would not have approved of any of his daughters making eyes at the choirboys but I got away with it.

From my earliest recollections I have always had an awareness of God's presence. If someone had asked me how I knew, I couldn't have told them. But deep, deep down I knew where this presence came from. It had been with me from the beginning, it was a permanent thing. Was this what I experienced at those magnificent, heavenly hideouts of natural beauty? Did I draw closer to God in these moments? Was this the reason I sought to be alone, out of sight, in silence; in an empty church, in the countryside. This wonderful something intensified and whirred up within me, growing stronger as I grew older. Was I, even at that early age, unknowingly longing to find the Lord? Was he drawing me to himself right from the very beginning? I cannot answer all those questions as I don't know and still don't know what took place in me during those wonderful moments. All I did know was that I never wanted these moments to fade away. In our church services that I found so dull, there was however just one sentence that filled me with awe, and took me over in an amazing way. From the prayer book service which we had in those days it said the following: 'We do not presume to come to this thy table O Lord trusting in our own righteousness.' What was it? It happened every time. But what happened? I seem to have been taken up into a something, somewhere which I could neither understand nor explain. Running parallel with the success of my budding music career, I realised I was becoming much more religious. Yes I use that word as, at that time, I felt more devout, I wanted to become better.

We were still attending the same dull church so when the vicar left, I left too. My parents weren't pleased. What shall we say to the new vicar, my father mentioned? That our daughter goes to one church and her parents to another. Quite frankly I didn't care, I got nothing from the one I was leaving and wanted to go to the parish church where there was a large congregation. I was accused of following the Man, and much worse the church was a higher one. Looking back I realise which Man I was following but then I had only got as far as the vicar.

On the shelf in my new bedroom I made a little holy place. I placed pretty cards with text on them with a wooden cross in the centre. I loved that shelf, it was precious to me. But nothing seemed personal; I was always reaching out at this something. I knew it was there but how could I get it? My search deepened. Now I had the overwhelming desire to read the Bible, I needed all the courage in the world to ask for one for my birthday or Christmas, I forget which. In our new church there were books, the daily Bible reading, and I just wanted to start reading them. What on earth the thoughts were in my family, especially after having had Grandma live with us and her example, I can't imagine but whatever they were nothing ever reached my ears. In time, I received a Bible and a prayer book. No doubt I was thought as going a bit overboard in that direction, now getting religious mania or something awful. Moderation in all things I had been taught.

Chapter 3

Do you remember the old type of gramophone, and the old type of records? There were three speeds weren't there: forty-five, seventy-eight, and thirty-three-and-a-third RPMs. When the record was placed on the central pivot, one had to be sure the speed was set correctly for the type of record on turntable, if not - disaster. The wrong speed for the wrong record made it either a high pitched babble, or a deep gruff inaudible sound. Whichever way, if the speed was incorrect, the record was mostly incomprehensible.

We had a special brush to remove any dust that might mar the reproduction; it was imperative that the record was kept clean, anything clogging the grooves, however small, would spoil it, blurring the performance. I remember there being three little tins of needles, each for the different speeds. On the lids, a dog sat listening to the sound on an old-fashioned hand-wound turntable. But all this was of little use unless the central pivot held the record firmly in place.

At the age of eighteen came my first spiritual encounter with God. It shook me to the core, and stopped me in my tracks. It was the first step that turned my life to face a completely new direction which ultimately led me to the decision to step onto God's Turntable. I was on holiday in Hythe, Kent at the time, staying with one of my sisters (Barbara) and her husband (Ralph), who lived in Seabrook Road. The previous day, we had had a pleasant trip taking the Romney Marsh Light Railway to Dungeness. I went to bed that night and, as far as I knew, everything was going to be just as it always had been. But the next morning when I awoke, my left arm was paralysed. It just wouldn't move. I then realised the left side of my face had been slightly affected too. I was terrified. The thought of being incapacitated and, worse still, my career and all the hoped for glory gone forever. As if that wasn't shattering enough, there was something else that brought me into a new reality. The 'presence' I'd known and felt all my life had taken on the form of a Person. I lay there face to face with God Himself!

Looking back, the wonderful thing was that I recognised Him immediately. There was no doubt in my mind who He was. In the light of Him, I saw the utter futility of all my efforts, ambitions and life so far. I saw that this supreme Person had the power not only to stop me in my tracks but also to let me remain in this condition for the rest of my life, and I had no power to change it. In His immensity, I saw my smallness, my nothingness. But my thoughts were selfish and self-centred. 'If You will heal me, I will serve You!' I said. I can hardly believe I had the nerve to demand, or even suggest such a request. As I lay there with all the time in the world to think, I struggled hard to see if there was any life left in my arm. Tensing my whole body in concentration, I willed my arm to move. I found it would suddenly lift up then collapse on the bed again. So there was still life in it I thought. I kept working on it throughout the day and over the next few weeks it came back to normal. My face was quickly right again so, in spite of my selfish, self-centred bargaining, the Lord answered my prayer, but I emerged from the experience a very changed person. And what of my side of the bargaining; did I keep it? Well, I tried. I knew of no other way except by trying to do what I thought would please Him.

Life went on more or less the same, except that now I prayed to a person. No one really knew what had happened, and why my arm suddenly became paralysed, the doctor couldn't explain it either. But I knew only too well. God had laid a very special hand on me for a very special work He had for me to do.

God, in my understanding, has a special work for each one of us already mapped out in eternity but so often we only want Him in our lives when it suits us. We grope on, wondering why we never find the happiness and satisfaction we'd hoped for. How many times does the Lord lay us down on a sick bed in order to get our attention? I tried so very hard to please Him, doing what I thought to be right. Now I know that all I did didn't make the slightest difference. He didn't want my good works, He wanted my life. But all that had yet to be shown to me as yet I hadn't met the wonderful person called Jesus.

I started going to seven o'clock communion on Sunday mornings instead of eight. Surely that must have pleased Him? Wasn't I making a grand effort? Not having studied the Bible, I had not heard that 'all your righteousness is as filthy rags.' Not very encouraging or complimentary words are they, when you are trying so hard to do your best to please someone, living as you think He would have you live. But I honestly and truly believed that at that time God was pleased with my supreme efforts, (and sacrifice in getting up an hour earlier on a Sunday). People said, 'aren't you good,' and yes, I believed them.

No indication had been given to me to stop my music studies, so I just continued. In July and December 1948 I passed with distinction the Royal Schools of Music grades VI and VII for singing. In the following May I took grade VIII, again passing with distinction and winning a silver medal, the second highest in Britain. I entered music festivals throughout the South of England with very promising remarks from the adjudicators. Singing oratorio was my greatest love, then Lieder. Opera didn't interest me in the slightest.

My singing teacher used to visit Winchester once a week; she booked a room over a music shop. There I went regularly, still with the hope of one day being a great singer. Apparently one day, so I was told, I was singing I know that my Redeemer Liveth from the Messiah when my teacher asked me outright if I understood what I was singing. I thought it over for a minute, and then said I didn't. She never explained there and then what it meant but later in the year I was invited to go with her to Eastbourne for a holiday retreat run by people called the Wood brothers. It was in fact the National Young Life Campaign. Would I like to come? Well, it seemed double-Dutch to me, nevertheless I said I would go. The year was 1953.

Crowds of young people were there. I remember that meals were served at very long tables, and the noise was terrible. Each morning there was a meeting, then again in the evening. The remainder of the day was free for us to go out and do what we liked. Of course, no one was compelled to attend the meetings but it was naturally expected for them to do so. In the afternoons we visited the town, went for walks above the cliffs, and a boat ride. The first thing I noticed during the meetings was that everybody, except me, seemed to be singing and praying to a real person. Although I now knew God to be a person, I just seemed to have standing in front of me a gigantic wall which I couldn't move, penetrate, or get around. We sang choruses and prayed, but I felt strangely out of it. It was all so different from anything I'd ever known before. Each of us had a little cell off a long dormitory where we slept. The tiny room had a bed, chair, table and a wardrobe.

After some days, I found myself praying a prayer I'd never prayed before, 'If You want me to make a decision, whatever that means, please send me a certain person, and I will accept that as a sign.' I really couldn't make anything out, except I knew I ought to make this decision. Others were making it, and it seemed the right thing for me to make it.

Out on a walk one afternoon, Mrs Wood came up and spoke to me about this decision business. Now I knew deep down I had to make it (a decision). But what was happening? Suddenly I was at war inside. I never wanted to speak to Mrs Wood again. I must avoid her. I became terrified. What was this tremendous thing I knew I had to do? Entrust my life to Someone I didn't know? Hadn't I been baptised, confirmed? Wasn't that enough? Why all this sudden emphasis about inviting this Jesus into my life? Who was He anyway? Help! Why had I ever come here in the first place; I was furious. I'd been caught in a trap. That's what it was, they had caught me in a trap whoever 'they' were. But I knew I had to go through with it, there was now no escape.

Next day, Mrs Wood was talking to me again on the subject. Oh, why can't she leave me alone? Can't she see what I'm going through? But I was caught alone in a room with her, and the door was closed. Oh God, I thought, now there is literally no escape. She asked me to pray but I didn't know what to say. I hadn't a clue. I was in such a whirl and muddle in my mind. I asked her to pray for me which she did. I don't remember what she said but I left the room trembling and sweating. Oh God, what made me come here? I felt sick and ill. Up in my cell, my nerves quietened.

Here I was alone, in silence. Now I had time to think. Picking up my daily reading, I read the heading 'Walk in the Light.' What on earth did it mean? I knelt on my knees by my bed, and poured out my heart in my own words to this Jesus that He would come into my life - come what may. It was done, at last. I had finally done it. But I was too bewildered to think what was involved. Only an instant peace and release had come into me. I climbed into bed, too tired even to care what the consequences would be, and fell asleep.

At some time during that night I was taken in spirit into what I believe must have been heaven itself. It was filled with a pure radiance of white light; it was a place of perfection, utter cleanness and beauty, like nothing I'd ever seen or could imagine. This light shone with a dazzling brilliance that was clean throughout. It was everywhere, yet in one place, and in the centre was a 'being' from whom this light radiated. I saw Him, yet not with earthly eyes. He had no shape or form as we know it, but I stood in the glory that issued from Him, filling that place. He approached me, yet He was already there, He took something from me, putting it behind Him. Immediately I felt a lightness of heart. I then saw what appeared like two doors opening outwards. From them, a long narrow pathway ran downhill into infinity. I stood at the top, as though on some pinnacle and saw something that resembled a curled up object rolling down the pathway, until it was out of sight. Then I heard a voice say, 'I have taken away your sins, Satan has no power over you.' Suddenly at this point I awoke, my soul bursting with indescribable joy. For a moment I couldn't grasp what had happened. It was now dawn. I leapt out of bed pinching myself. Was I really still me? I felt like another person. Oh yes, I felt the pinch, it was me all right. Walking to the window in absolute wonder and amazement, I looked out. There, high in the sky was a cross; gloriously shining with the same wondrous light I'd seen in that place. I stared and stared at it, until clouds covered it over. When they had passed, the cross was no longer to be seen. I then realised the wall that had stood before me was completely gone.

I was a changed person, completely taken out of myself! How I longed to go back to that wonderful place, but I knew there was work for me to do. I wanted to tell the world what had happened that night of 25 August 1953 but no one wanted to believe me. There was no moderation about this experience. Not only had I gone completely overboard, but I had also become totally committed. I had stepped on to God's Turntable!

Has it ever seemed strange to you that so many people want to see into their future, when they can't even cope with what is just a nose-length away? Why do we want to know? What difference will it make? Would you really want to know what misfortune or disaster lurks around the corner? Perhaps you only want to know the exciting things that will happen.

Does the thought of being a failure lie behind it all? If we could see aright, would we walk aright? People turn to so many things don't they? Fortune telling, handwriting, stars, almost anything in which they believe they can get guidance concerning the future. Mercifully, God in His wisdom has hidden the future from us, and for a good reason. Would you want to foresee a terrible disaster or accident that could maim you for life? Or foresee the loss of someone you love dearly? What state of mind would you be in on the day you knew it was going to happen?

If I had been shown in advance what lay ahead for me personally, after making that decision to step onto God's Turntable, I would have stepped off in a great hurry. How I thank the Lord that He never let me see the way He intended to take me. Had He, I would have turned my back on Him and walked away, making the excuse that the sacrifice involved was far too great, and that I wasn't prepared to go that extra mile He expects us to go willingly. The Lord does not want 'some' thing or 'part' of us. He wants 'everything' and the 'whole' of us. Therein lays the cost, therein lays the sacrifice. It is a colossal cost, and a colossal sacrifice. It is literally all; one hundred percent. The whole question is; are we willing?

The guidance I've received throughout my life had been one step at a time, one day at a time. In later years, I saw the wisdom of it. I would never have been able to get through some of the things He asked me to go through had I seen them all in advance.

Chapter 4

When I was about fifteen years old, my father was diagnosed as having diabetes. His health had been his pride and joy; he was a robust man, full of vigour, vitality, humour and life. He never fully recovered from this blow, slowly sliding downhill in every way. Ten years later, on 3 January 1955, he died at the age of sixty-three.

Age 23: Shirley with parents at Winchester, 1951

Our home in Winchester was now sold. My three sisters had already left home; my eldest sister (Monica) had left to become a nurse, the second (Barbara) had joined the WAAFS and the third (Audrey) had become a Voluntary Aid Detachment nurse during wartime. By 1955, Barbara and Audrey had already married. I was the last of the sisters at home. On Daddy's death, Mummy moved to Bexhill-on-Sea, and I to Bournemouth to continue my singing lessons with the lady who visited Winchester, but who lived on the coast. I now had to think about earning my living. Never knowing what I wanted to do except become a singer, I had not had any other training except singing. However, I applied for an advertised live-in job as a ward maid at a convalescent home and was accepted. My average working day was as follows.

I got up around 6 am to prepare the early morning tea for the patients and staff. It took me roughly an hour to get dressed and organised by 7 am. In a corner not far from my room was a gas burner, tripod in shape which, to my mind, stood most precariously on a triangular shelf. On this I placed a large brown kettle filled with water. I then had to fetch milk from the basement. I could have used the lift at the other end of the corridor but it made such a noise I was afraid of waking up the whole household so down three flights of stairs I went, the back stairs of course. In a fridge in the huge larder was the milk. For a time - until their breeding place was found and dealt with - the basement was home to hundreds of cockroaches. I was the first to greet them after their night of revelry. Having descended two flights of stairs, I would push open the swing door from the hall, check on the time from the clock; then creep along the darkish passage to the top of the last flight of stairs. The basement was in complete darkness and when I switched on the light a black clicking-clacking mass could be seen racing in all directions. There were grandpas and grandmas, nephews, nieces, brothers, sisters, cousins, offspring of diverse sizes, and most assuredly expectant mothers, to be seen scuttling for their lives under the wainscoting and into nooks and crannies. Before I'd counted ten, I was all alone in the basement. Taking the milk from the fridge, I climbed two flights of stairs again, leaving the milk jug on the table outside the patients' bedrooms. There was always someone up by then so I left them to pour it into the beakers. By the time I'd arrived at the top of the third flight, I was usually just in time to take the kettle off the gas burner before the water boiled over onto the floor. The ration of tea for each morning, in little empty fish-paste jars, was duly put into a very large aluminium teapot, the boiling water added, and the kettle refilled with water and replaced on the burner. I now had to carry the huge teapot down a flight of stairs, resting it on a stair to open the door onto the patients' corridor. By now, many patients were up and waiting for me with their tongues hanging out. I always poured the tea, as the pot was very heavy. Certainly I'm sure there would be objection these days if an employee was asked to carry such a huge teapot.

Upstairs again I went to rescue the second kettle of water, and make tea for the staff. On a small tray holding a teapot and milk jug, I walked to where the staff had their rooms. Politely knocking on the bedroom doors, I entered when the command of 'come in' was vaguely heard from the depths of bedclothes and hairnets.

'Good morning,' I said brightly to the sleepy faces with half-opened eyes topped with wonky curlers pushing at the hairnets. I filled up their cups (no beakers here), then quietly retreated, not backwards. A moment's pause for my own sip of tea, then donning a plum-coloured overall, I carried the second kettle full of boiling water down the flight of stairs to the patients, for those who wanted seconds.

Along the end of the corridor was my cupboard where the cleaning things were kept. Taking everything I needed, I went to the sitting rooms on the ground floor where there was just enough time for me to clean one of the rooms: sweep the carpets, mop the lino, dust and polish the chairs and tables, empty the wastepaper baskets; then hurray, 8 am breakfast!

I had half an hour for breakfast and a very good one it was, eaten of course in the basement where the kitchen, sculleries and staff dining-rooms were located. Naturally, we domestic staff never ate with the nursing staff. We were servants, they were ladies. After my breakfast, I went upstairs to make my bed. While the patients had their breakfast at 9 am, the nurses made the beds. Then in our plum-coloured ward maid's uniforms we swooped, the both of us, to start the cleaning of these very large rooms; most had five beds in them. The floors were covered with lino and small slip mats between the beds. Each patient had a wardrobe and a dressing-table with three drawers. Everything was cleaned by hand, the hard way. I vaguely remember the presence of a Hoover but my 'mate' and I shared a carpet-sweeper or, as I did more often than not, shake the mats outside on the large balcony. Floors were swept or mopped.

Putting the polish on the floors was done on hands and knees; we used a heavy bumper which took considerable effort to push back and forth, and it took considerable time before the lino began to shine. Finally, the furniture was polished and dusted. When the other ward maid had her day off, I had all her work to do in addition to mine; she in turn did all my work on my day off. We received no extra pay or thanks for it, and it all had to be done in the same time as we did our normal morning's allotted duties. We had half an hour for lunch, then were back to work again, finishing what hadn't been completed, usually the bathrooms. By 4.30 pm the work was finished.

It never took me until the end of the afternoon to complete my bathrooms so I often sat by a window looking out. But there were always spies around. Through a crack in an open door, you could see a nurse creeping over the carpet to surprise you at work. But not me; I knew where to place the chair by the window to have a full view of the crack in the door. I would leave all my floor cloths and polish strewn on the floor so that, as I saw a spy approach, I would be on my knees in a flash, polishing ever so hard. One day, I saw a particular nurse approach so I hid behind the door and, as she reached it, I called through the crack, 'did you want me nurse?' That cured this particular spy, but there were still others. Sometimes I finished work at 2 pm and began again at 5 pm to help serve supper in the patients' dining-room.

On arrival in the evening, the first job was to clear the tea things away and stack them on a trolley. The trolley was then wheeled into a lift and taken down to the basement scullery. There were no dishwashers then; it was all just plain hard work. When everything had been washed, dried, and re-stacked onto the trolley, it was wheeled back into the lift and taken upstairs. The tables were then laid for supper. If someone hadn't put the hall clock on five minutes, to get finished earlier, the patients ate at 6.30 pm, and not at 6.25 pm. We hauled the food up from the kitchen on a hand-pulled lift, placing it on top of a hot plate oven. The Sister on duty did the serving while two of us, an orderly and I, raced around with the loaded plates to the tables. We paused until the patients had finished or had been given second helpings, and then collected the empty plates, stacking them on the trolley standing in the hall. Now it was the pudding's turn to be hauled up on the hand lift. This also was served onto hot dishes and away we went again, trying to be gracious and not appear to be in a hurry.

When everyone had finished, grace was said with all speed and no meaning, and Sister departed from our presence. Then began a real race against time. We had to clear the tables, trying not to push the patients over as they slowly left the dining-room, stack everything on the trolley, wheel it into the lift; that is if no one had taken it upstairs and left the doors open, (not deliberately surely?) and get it into the scullery by 7 pm. Why? The sisters and evening staff came down at the sound of a bell for their supper, and it was for me to wait on them.

Ding-dong; down came the ladies who trouped into their own dining-room while I loaded a very large and heavy metal tray with delicate dishes of this and that. If their door had been left open it made all the difference, and life was much easier, as I didn't have to balance the tray on my knees so I could open it by myself. All was genteelly set before them, then for a wild dash back to the scullery to clear the back-log of washing up. One had to judge the time it took the ladies to eat their first course, like ladies; then off I shot to the kitchen for the second course. Once again, the tray made its way on distended biceps to their dining-room, dirties were cleared off the table, sometimes a thank you - more often not, then dessert was set before them. A second dash back to the scullery usually completed the washing up. Now the trolley was ready for its last upward journey of the day.

Up we went in the lift, setting the tables for breakfast, putting all that wasn't required back in the cupboards. The evening's work was almost finished, only the staff dining-room to re-set, as the cooks graciously did their own washing up. If the unsuspected clock had not been found out, we finished five minutes earlier! The only items remaining on my agenda were supper and then to bed.

Once a year we spring cleaned. Walls were washed, and floors scrubbed. It was a back-breaking job, done on our knees with a tablet of soap and a scrubbing brush. Three of us did it, as the dining-room maid also lent a hand. We knelt on the floor in a row, scrubbing in a straight line, until every huge room was eventually done. When the floors were dry, they were re-polished, with us again on hands and knees. Then, if we had any energy left which we were expected to have, we pushed and pulled the heavy bumpers back and forth until the floors shone like glass. The floor polish we used was an orange colour and rather oily. Once a week we were given a ration which had to last the whole week. If, for some reason, it didn't, we were told not to be so extravagant, or asked 'What have you done with it?' If someone ran out, she didn't hesitate to take someone else's. I had to hide some of my supplies in my room, so that no one could pinch them. Anyway, how did 'they' know how much we needed? They never did the work. They only inspected, criticised, or sometimes complimented. What made 'them' think 'they' knew?

What a contrast to the life I'd hitherto known. Already God's Turntable had gone a full circle, with me on it. No longer was I on the receiving end, but on the giving end. 'Let he that will be greatest among you, be the servant of all.' Very easily preached, but not so easily produced. It was in this job that I found out I was a snob.

Those years were a living hell. Never had I worked so hard, been so insulted, experienced such disappointment and disillusionment. Also, matters of the heart were in full swing which didn't help either. It's one thing coping with your head but quite another coping with your heart. I also saw the door to a singing career slowly closing. My heart was breaking in more than one direction. The joy I'd once known seemed all too soon faded and gone, and I felt I'd fallen into one of the deepest, most terrifying pits I'd ever known. I didn't believe I'd ever rise up out of it. I held fast to what I already knew, praying on that knowledge, and battled on with my quiet times. There followed one heartbreak after another. I got over one hurdle, only to fall flat on my face before the next one. I felt caught in an awful trap with no way of escape. There was now no vision to uplift me, and usually by the evening I wept bitter tears from despair and physical exhaustion. Where was the Lord who had done such wondrous things for me? I felt He had gone, but deep in my heart I knew He was still there in spite of it all.

Although my life at that time was so heartbreakingly severe in its struggle, there came times that were lovely which I told no one about. The two occasions I'm about to recount were the beginning of my rising up out of that dreadful pit.

I studied the organ in Bournemouth and was allowed to practise in one of the churches. To this day, it remains my favourite instrument. One afternoon, while I was practising, it was as though an electric current suddenly shot clean through my body from head to foot. I stopped playing, unable to make out what had happened, when it happened again. A few seconds later, I experienced yet another shot. It was an ecstatic experience. I felt I'd received power of some kind. Even to this day, I still don't know what it was.

The second episode happened in the convalescent home. Flu had gone around the staff, and now it was my turn. On waking one morning, although I felt so ill, I was not considered sick enough to stay in bed. I dragged my aching body out of bed, wishing I lived out so that I could have stayed in bed without having to ask permission. Deep down, I was aware of an inner excitement that something was going to happen. At ten past eleven, I was cleaning in one of the bedrooms when it filled with a 'glory.' I became rooted to the spot, electrified in some sort of way. It was like an electric shock that shot through my entire body. A second later, I realised I had been cured from flu. It had literally gone.

None of us likes losing face or having to apologise do we? Especially if we are sure we are right? What a problem this is, and what misery we suffer because of it. Great misunderstandings arise, simply because neither side is prepared to lose face and admit they could have been wrong. It's always the other person's fault isn't it? But on God's Turntable there are many agonising grooves we have to travel. I had arrived in one of them.

When I cleaned the patients' bedrooms my method was to fill the wastepaper baskets with any rubbish that was to be thrown away, then during our tea break take them with me to the basement, emptying them outside in the dustbins. At least it saved me one journey in the course of the day. I must have walked miles in that home.

After the tea break, I took the baskets back upstairs, leaving them outside the bedrooms until they were finished, then I put them back inside each room. I sang a lot while I went about my work, quietly of course. This was not because I was deliriously happy with my lot, far from it, but it did help me get through the day with a slightly lighter heart.

Imagine how I reacted when I came out and found the baskets full of rubbish again. I knew immediately who had done it; one of the nurses. I exploded into an uncontrollable rage. This was the last straw. I had just about had enough of being spoken to rudely, sneaked upon, talked at and treated as if I were just a lump of dirt to function at someone else's beck and call, and now this. I stormed along the corridor, blasting out at the guilty nurse, in a fury that was quite shattering. I trembled and shook with uncontrollable rage. The nurse paid no attention whatsoever which made me even madder. What my blood pressure must have been I just can't imagine. Whenever I passed the nurse, I tossed my head and cut her through with all the airs and graces I could muster. I doubt if she even noticed though. Actually, I suffered terribly, and was deeply unhappy for three days; I couldn't eat or sleep. But it was her fault. She made me lose my temper. I was the persecuted one. I was the innocent party. I was the offended one. The way I was sailing about, no one would have thought I had done anything wrong at all.

However, during those three terrible days, something rather unexpected happened. It came as a 'still small voice,' whispering something very quietly and very deeply in my heart, which I hated and didn't want to hear. The voice said, 'You are to apologise.'

'Never, never, never,' I yelled back. 'It's not fair and you know it. She had no right to put her rotten rubbish in my baskets. I won't be taken advantage of. I won't give in. I won't apologise.'

But the voice hadn't finished speaking to me. 'You lost your temper. For that reason only I want you to apologise.' So it had nothing to do with who I thought was right or wrong. I had lost my temper and that in itself was wrong.

'No, had she not done what she did, I would not have had to get mad and lose my temper. It was still her fault. She'd made me lose my temper.' But what was this I was now hearing? I had chosen of my own free will to lose my temper. What utter rubbish! I'm certainly not going to believe that. I refuse to apologise because I know I'm in the right. 'It's all her fault,' I continued pigheadedly. So the unhappy days continued, until the burden of disobedience became so great, and I knew I had to get it over and done with. A great heaviness had taken over. Each day was worse than the last. It was the weight that was getting me down.

On the third day, I knew I could stand it no longer so I made up my mind early that morning that I must apologise. It was a terrible day. I put the apology off time and again. As far as I was concerned I was still in the right. Later during the morning, I saw the nurse at the other end of the corridor. Before I had time to change my mind, I tore up to her snapping out in the most ungracious and bitter tone, 'I'm sorry I lost my temper the other day.' Inwardly, I wasn't in the least bit sorry.

I pursed my lips together so they couldn't open as I heard her say in an equally superior tone to the one I had used, 'Well, I did wonder what it was all about.' I felt myself turn crimson with rage, but suddenly at peace inside. I had done it. It was over. As I calmed down, there came the most wonderful inner peace and tranquillity. To think I had suffered all that time, simply because I was too proud to admit I also was at fault. But until that time, I was spiritually blind, now I was beginning to see with other eyes of understanding. Before I left the home, the nurse and I became the best of friends. She never did anything like that again.

Bournemouth in the 50s

On the Sunday mornings I had off, I went to Lansdowne Baptist Church for the services which were always packed out. The sermons (if one could call them that) went on for forty-five minutes or more. I lost all sense of time during those wonderful Bible studies we received from the minister. It was a real grounding in the scriptures which I'm sure helped me come through so much that was so heartbreakingly difficult then. It was while I attended this church, that I knew I had to go through the waters of baptism.

I had been eight years old when christened in Winchester; why so late I'm not sure. So why did I feel I should be baptised by immersion? It wasn't so much a feeling but something I knew the Lord wanted me to do. As so many young people were baptised in that church, one might have felt it was the done thing, compelling me to do it also but this was not the case. To me, there was something very significant about being buried with Him through baptism into death in order that, just as Christ was raised from the dead through the glory of the Father, we too may live a new life. (Rom. 6:4).

I knew this was only symbolic, that the actual waters themselves would not give me new life but somehow the fact of being completely immersed meant I was taking on myself what had been taken on by others when I was christened. I had committed myself to the Lord when I stepped onto his Turntable. Now I wanted to be identified with Him, and in this way I believed He was telling me openly to take this step before the world as it were. I was publicly identifying myself with Him. On the same evening that I was baptised, there were a lot of others taking the same step. We usually gave a short testimony then stepped into the water where the minister and another man were waiting for us. The fact that I have always been frightened of my head going under water never entered my mind. It was a glorious experience, and I've always been glad I did what I knew the Lord wanted me to do.

In 1958, I moved into a bed-sitter in a friend's house not far away (in Bournemouth). Living-in, one never gets away from the job, even on days off. I was beginning to get tired of this. Already I'd acquired a little furniture; a small round oak table plus two chairs, one being a rocker. They cost around £6 each. I also bought a small record player. In the evenings, I'd sit listening to it - Beethoven's Eroica symphony was my favourite - while I did my embroidery. Every time I've heard that symphony played since, my mind goes back to that room, and the piece of embroidery I was doing at that time. Likewise, I can play piano pieces I haven't played in years and I'm immediately transported back to when I studied them. What a wonderful thing the mind is.

I never kept a record of how much we were paid in those days, not much in comparison with pay rates tody but I do recall going out and buying three lovely dresses in one go. They cost £5 each; what an extravagance.

One 14 June 1959 my eldest sister (Monica) and I flew to Austria for a holiday. It was my first flight, and my first trip abroad. I made a few notes of the trip at the time in my diary, but nothing in great detail. What I do remember most vividly was that I fell in love with the country. Never had I seen such mountains and fields with their magnificent display of wild flowers, as our walks took us up the mountains and treks from village to village. Cows with their bells hanging around their necks; sudden downbursts of rain, followed by brilliantly hot sunshine; walking through clouds of vapour that made one cold and damp; hot fresh rolls with strawberry jam and coffee for breakfast; views of unsurpassed beauty. Two weeks in that lovely country made me yearn for mountains with snow on them ever since. I felt I belonged there and deep in my heart I knew I would return one day. With this foreknowledge, I bought books on the German language and began to study them. In my plum-coloured overalls pocket, I kept an ever increasing list of words which I learned during the afternoons when I was on duty, sitting by the bathroom window, watching the crack in the door for spies. I was to wait twelve years before being guided to go back and live in Austria.

Slowly though in Bournemouth, I became aware that the door was closing at the convalescent home. In one of my quiet times I had the assurance of this through the following verse: Isaiah 42:16. 'I will lead the blind by ways they have not known; along unfamiliar paths I will guide them. I will turn the darkness into light before them and make the rough places smooth. These are the things I will do. I will not forsake them.'

I knew the place to be a large one, much larger than I'd ever known, but where and when I had no idea. Two years later I did take wings to that 'large place;' on 4 September 1959, I walked out of the convalescent home for the last time. The Lord had finally closed the door. There weren't any goodbyes, and I'm sure I didn't shed any tears. For four years and eight months I'd been in that crucible. Quite long enough.

I moved my bits and pieces to stay with my sister and her husband (Barbara and Ralph) in Hythe, Kent, until some months later when I moved to a flat in Cheriton Road, Folkestone. I'd found work; in an old peoples' home!

Grandma had died (in 1953, age 94), leaving us all a small amount of money; with it, I furnished the flat in Folkestone with the intention of staying. But staying was not on the Turntable; not for me at any rate. God had other plans for me. I would be on the move for another twenty-four years.

While I'd lived in Bournemouth, I had been trying to keep up with my singing but problems had mounted. Firstly, I couldn't find a place to practise and I was usually too tired by the end of the day to sing. Somehow things dragged on although, as I've previously mentioned, I knew the door was closing on a singing career. Living in Folkestone, I still tried to keep the door open. I auditioned with a well-known teacher in London but each lesson was terribly expensive, far beyond my pocket, and every attempt to have one seemed to get more and more difficult. It was now autumn and either fog or train delays made me cancel the lessons. Again, it also became increasingly difficult to find somewhere to practise. In one heart-breaking moment, after four months of struggling, I sat on the floor alone in my flat and, with tears streaming down my face, gave up the struggle, admitting defeat. Yes, I had to let go of my 'first love,' because now there was Someone else who wanted me to 'love Him more than this.' From that moment on, I can say honestly that He has been my 'only love.'

Portrait of Shirley, age 26, taken at Beaconsfield House, Winchester, in 1954 by her father, shortly before he died

The moment I let go, the most marvellous peace flooded my heart. This, plus the relief of ending the struggle, outweighed the personal loss. Looking back, I find it incredible that I really believed I had the power to keep that door open if I worked hard enough at it. It had also become clear to me that I had a serving ministry and, except for a few other types of jobs very occasionally, this continued to remain so.

In Folkestone, I worked with some very nice people, cleaning of course. I earned 2s 6p an hour in those days, and the rent for my flat was £8 a month. It was as hard then to make ends meet as it has always been. Had I been paid 3s an hour, I would have been in clover. The trouble was there was no clover in Folkestone at that time. No-one wanted to employ me on a Monday as they would have had to contribute to the weekly welfare stamp towards my old age pension. I literally had to plead with people to employ me on a Monday, otherwise I had to pay for the stamp myself, and for me that was a lot of money. Finally, I found two jobs on Mondays, so at least the stamp cost was divided between two people. It was while I worked for one of these ladies (on a Monday) that the 'large place' referred to in the verse given to me two years previously was pin-pointed. 'Why don't you migrate to America? There are so many opportunities there for young people,' I was told. Immediately, this was confirmed in my heart. This was the place where I had to go. I was wild with excitement at the thought of going to the United States. Had I been able to see ahead, I would have backed out, stepping clean off the Turntable. All I thought of was the marvellous things that would happen after I got there. Little did I know!

I applied to the American Embassy for a visa, then had all the necessary papers to fill in, plus references etc, etc. I was going out as a kind of au pair (a bit of an old one), so a family to employ me had to be found in advance. Eventually one agreed to have me, and advanced the fare, which I would pay back over a course of a year's employment. When everything was finalised, I was told to go to the embassy to receive my visa. On arrival, a quick medical told me I was in excellent health. Over a desk, I stood with my right hand raised, declaring I had no intention of overthrowing the government (how I would have set about it I really couldn't imagine), and forthwith, was handed my visa. This, however, was no time for frivolities; I became sick with nerves. What was I doing? What would happen? From deep within, as though I had been forewarned, I knew I was heading for trouble. My last question at the embassy before I left was: 'Can the contract be broken if I don't like the family?'

Oh yes it could be, 'providing you reimburse the family the money they have advanced for your fare.' Cold comfort seeing that I now had so little. Giving some of my furniture to my sister and selling the remainder, all thoughts of settling down flew out of the window.

My air ticket arrived; the day and time of departure was 23 May 1962 at 7.25 pm. Mummy and I went to my other married sister Audrey in Croydon where we spent the night before the great day. As I was still sick with nerves, my doctor brother-in-law gave me a sleeping pill to quieten me down. I slept like the dead, if the dead sleep. The problem was waking up. My head was so heavy; I felt I was going to my own funeral not to the United States. Secretly, I was terrified. What if that forewarning was correct? What should I do? Tears were just around the corner where they often are.

Mummy, my sister and I set out for London Airport, as it was then called and, as we drew nearer, we watched the huge jets coming in to land. It seemed they were just above our heads; the thrill that I would soon be in one helped combat my fears. As we piled out of a taxi, it became apparent that my suitcase was far too big to handle. (I soon learned never to travel with anything I couldn't manage. The main problem for me was that, being so short, I can't carry a suitcase with my arms straight. Instead, I have to carry them with arms bent.

Eventually, the call came to board the Boeing 707 and amid goodbyes and tears I passed through the final barrier. As I did so, the most ghastly feeling came over me. All security I'd ever known was left behind. That barrier was the division between having someone to help me if needed, and having no-one to turn to at all. Only God knew what I was doing. I certainly didn't. I felt so ill I wanted to wake up and find it was all just a hideous dream.

Looking back, I've lost count of the times I've gone out not knowing where I was going. Oswald Chambers in his book, *My Utmost for His Highest*, puts this very clearly:

> 'You did not choose me, but I chose you to go and bear fruit - fruit that will last' - (John 15: 16 NIV - New International Version)
>
> 'We are not taken up into conscious agreement with God's purpose; we are taken up into God's purpose without any consciousness at all. We have no conception of what God is aiming at and, as we go on, it gets more and more vague. God's aim looks like missing the mark because we are too short-sighted to see what He is aiming at.'

I had launched out into the deep and was letting down my nets. This was the first of so many launches and I think the hardest. Although I knew who my Leader was, I had yet to learn to trust Him. He had to increase my faith. In my extremity was His opportunity, to prove to me He had prepared the way before me in spite of the vagueness of each step. I had to learn I did not walk alone, but how else could He prove that to me unless I launched out into the deep and let down my net with my own hands? He didn't keep me from the depths but rescued me while I was in them.

I think that by the time you've read this book you will agree that what I caught in my nets was the most wonderful thing I, or you, could ever have netted.

Directly I stepped on to God's Turntable, and allowed Him to record His life in mine, I was quick to find out that I was to be involved with His Timetable. Seeing His ways are neither our ways, nor His thoughts nor our thoughts. I soon learned His timing is not our timing. The 'turn' and the 'time' must always coincide. There is always a reason behind which speed He chooses to use. Too fast or too slow could break and wreck the record and the recording. Everything must be perfectly timed and tuned. We may not always be timed in, but the Lord helps us when we are not tuned in. It is like a record with nothing on it; you may think He's forgotten because things go so slowly; but he hasn't. Many an obstacle is avoided by going at a very slow speed. It is not cruel testing, but the patient waiting of our loving Father until we are in the right place at the right time to move into the next groove. No jumping is allowed.

The Turntable turns slowly but steadily, always in the same direction; forwards, toward the central pivot which holds the record in place. We, none of us, know how long or how short our records will be, and they may turn at 45 rpm, or only 33 $^{1}/_{3}$. That matters very little, and is really of no importance; it's what has been recorded on them that matters; and don't forget, one day they will be played back to us, whether you believe it or not. Will we want to listen?

Chapter 5

The waiting seemed an eternity but eventually we were bumping down the runway until that magical moment of becoming airborne. Higher and higher we climbed into the heavens while smaller and smaller grew the country of my birth. We were soon flying at 32,000 ft. It was already getting dark when I left London but now, as we headed west, every minute brought more and more daylight; we seemed to fly back through a sunset until it was broad daylight again. How very odd!

Midnight English-time came and it was still daylight. I felt I was in a heavenly hideout, in the midnight sun! Would the day ever come to an end? Well it did, that elusive sunset came too; a blood red sun sliding down behind a blackened earth

Soon, way below out of nowhere, the lights of Newfoundland twinkled in the dark ... 3.40 am, we circled Idlewild Airport (later re-named Kennedy Airport) and I had arrived in my new world, heart pounding. My suitcase was searched, papers inspected, but where was my vaccination card? Not in my handbag as I thought. Panic blocked any recall, only random rummaging eventually found it.

Oh God, if I felt ill when I left London, I was now ready to die. I dreaded taking the next step in case the forewarning I had received was correct. But a man from my agency met me; and away we drove in his car, tyres screeching, past skyscrapers ablaze with lights. After it all – leaving England, saying goodbyes, the flight, gaining five hours, and arriving in a strange new place – I was exhausted, my nerves were tense and never had I felt so alone and frightened; and unsure. Had it really happened? Was I really in New York?

By my new time, it was around midnight (again) when we arrived in Maplewood, New Jersey. On being introduced to the lady of the house, a Mrs White, my fears were confirmed. I knew I could never last long in such a place. Dear God help me, I cried inwardly, what shall I do? Having asked for a cup of tea, I was told where everything was. I then proceeded to search for the required items in dozens of cupboards. Mrs White never rose from her chair; such opulence, such magnificence. Never had I seen the like of it. So ornate, so rich was the decor. The house was like a palace. While I drank my cup of tea, I was told my duties for the next day, and that I could stay in bed one hour later in the morning as 'no doubt you are tired after your long journey.' Tired? When the welcome tea had been drunk, I was shown to my living quarters. A door was opened leading to the basement. So this was to be my palace. For one year? What horror; it couldn't have been worse if I had been led into a prison.

From my diary:

'The only window, on ground level, approximately 22 ins X 24 ins, is the only light for the bedroom. Later I learned I could never open it as all the car fumes came in from the driveway. The ceiling is festooned with pipes! My bed is comfortable. Beside it stands an old bedside table, with a lamp minus a shade. The fixture is so wobbly I think my end is coming every time I turn it on and off! A shocking wardrobe with clothes in it already and a chest of drawers are at my disposal. Two bathmats have been laid on the floor.

'Out from the bedroom, to get to the toilet, I walk through a large area with boilers, rows of washing lines, old boxes, and piles of old rags. Everywhere, there is this strange odour. I will learn that the 'Lord of the palace' is in the meat slaughtering trade. Need I say more?

'In another section, they are like rooms without doors, are fridges, a washing machine, dryer, sinks, old bottles, plants, brooms and general mess.

'My sitting-room comprises one large room with a bar at one end, a TV, ironing board and iron, an old dilapidated couch, and a table covered with brilliant Formica. Hurray, two windows. The dust lies in rolls.'

Had I left England for this? Not likely. Already I knew what to do after a few days.

Up from the servants' quarters next morning, I entered the 'palace.' I noticed only half the downstairs was in use, the rest obviously being for show. Magnificent Marley tiled floors awaited my bended knees and working hands. Gold fitted carpets; couldn't be. Mahogany tables with chairs upholstered in turquoise. Chandeliers hung from the ceilings, dripping their magnificence. Chairs were covered in plastic to protect their sumptuousness. Even the lamps with fancy shades were wrapped in plastic. You mean to say there wasn't a spare shade for my lamp which didn't have one? What a lot of silver about. I wondered if I would ever get it all polished.

Retracing my steps into the dream kitchen of built-in cupboards, curtains and matching wallpaper, lights of fantastic shape and design, I saw nothing out of place, not a spot of dirt anywhere. No doubt the 'maid' will find something to do, somewhere, to occupy her short stay.

Up the stairs I went to the 'ladies' chambers. Exquisite curtains, couches, beds, carpets, furniture, drawers bulging with belongings, wash-basins, baths, toilets, tables, chairs, lamps, mirrors, object d'art everywhere. Oh no, not another flight of stairs? Oh yes, to the attic, if you care to come with me. Can I believe what I am seeing: a clothes shop in the attic? 'Why so many clothes?' the maid dares to ask the lady of the palace.

'We're sick of them', comes the reply.

Madam was openly pleased with her new maid. She had shown great concern the night of her arrival that it was a large house, but windows only had to be washed once a week and, yes, the silver cleaned as well. She inquired if the maid had seen a vacuum cleaning before? I thought I had somewhere. That was obviously a relief, as it saved her the trouble of explaining how it worked. Washing and ironing was to be kept up daily, bathrooms cleaned - and cleared - and of course, the same for the entire house.

She felt sure that if I rose at 6 am, breakfast would be ready for her family by 7 am. Good gracious, the bacon wasn't cooked correctly and where was the orange juice that had to be drunk daily for vitamins. So many different shaped spoons for so many different shaped bowls and mouths and, if the wrong spoon went with the wrong bowl, how the mouths moved. Bread to be cut, toast to be made; as fast as it was made it was consumed, and in no time at all the consumers departed for work, leaving only chaos to be cleared and cleaned.

I was informed my day off would start only after I had followed up behind the children, made the beds, cleared up their mess, folded the clothes and found room in the bulging drawers, done the washing up etc, etc. Madam didn't rise until late owing to the early hours to which she played bridge or whatever.

'But the contract says one full day off a week!'

'But this is America!'

'Really!'

I saw no need for argument. Her fate was sealed. When should I tell her? At last she had the girl she had been waiting for. She was so proud of her, so polite, even though she had come from some backward area of the globe called England. But had she been an early riser, she would have seen a small figure hurrying out of her yard at 5.45 am, carrying a letter in her hand addressed to the agency saying, 'get me out of here!'

Sunday came. Madam was planning a vacation. I would be around all day (and no doubt all night if needed) to cook, to clear, to clean, and to care for her family who as yet had not been taught to cook, clean, nor alas, to care.

The maid stood facing the kitchen sink. 'I shall not be staying here,' she said.

But what could be wrong? Such a beautiful home, I was selfish, foolish, this was America. Didn't I know when I was well off? Apparently not! 'You won't get anywhere by moving about!'

Well, how does anyone get anywhere without moving about? I ask you! With dignity, the maid stood motionless with her back to the sink, staring at the lady of the palace. Madam grew uncomfortable. She tried to reason with this girl from the old world.

Next day the agency was contacted. 'Take her away, I don't want her here!'

'Just one moment please, let me speak to her,' said a voice from the agency.

'Pick up the phone in one of the bedrooms,' my orders boomed. But one of the phones in one of the bedrooms had been at one of my ears for quite a time already. I made a noise, hoping it sounded as if I were just lifting the receiver.

'Hello!'

'Hi, what's the matter?'

'The basement!'

'The basement?'

'Yes, the basement, my living quarters!'

There was little or no packing to do, as I hadn't unpacked. The next day I was quietly removed from the 'palace.'

The relief I felt after leaving blotted from my mind the fact that I owed the family the fare they had advanced for me. Already two weeks had passed since my arrival in the United States. I felt utterly lost and alone in the world. The agency didn't know what to do with me, and I had exactly three dollars in my pocket. 'Can you type?' I was asked. The answer was 'no.'

'Pity, we could have employed you.' I was now out on a limb.

Could I trust and believe that God had not left me, nor forsaken me? I remembered the forewarning I had so clearly received at the embassy. Surely, if He had known this was going to happen, He must have planned what was to follow. How little I could guess that in a matter of a few hours the Lord was going to start showing me, and has shown me ever since, that not only did He know the road I was taking but had also provided for the journey. This was the start of my faith growing.

The agency took me plus baggage to a motel where I was shown into a twin-bedded room. I had no idea who would foot the bill. In fact I flatly refused to consider it. But doubt did begin to creep into my mind. What an idiot I am, I thought. Putting my suitcase down, I noticed in the centre of the table there were sachets of coffee, tea, dried milk and sugar. Ah, I thought, at least I shan't go thirsty. All facilities were there, kitchen, fridge, toilet, shower. Could this all be free? Going to the fridge and opening the door, there before me was a loaf of bread, and some butter. So I shan't starve either, I thought. And there was peace and quiet. No radios. Now I knew I wasn't alone at the mercy of the world but a loving Father was indeed providing every step of the way.

A few days later, I was informed my room was booked, so I was taken by the motel's owners to their summer cottage in the country. They mentioned that, if I liked to clean it out, they would pay me five dollars. I was more than happy to do it. But as night approached, I became terrified. There was I, right out in the heart of this new country quite alone – humanly speaking – with only the company of croaking frogs in a nearby pond. Now it was me who played the radio until midnight to calm my fears. Actually, the radio didn't do what I expected it to do as, when I switched it off and got into bed, the fears were still there. It just made me feel less isolated. I've since learned that perpetual noise is only a cover for deep needs underneath. Later during the early hours, I woke hearing my name called two or three times. 'Shirley, Shirley.' I leapt out of bed and saw the motel owner through the window. She had become so frightened at leaving me alone that she had driven out to the cottage to rescue me. I was bundled into her car and taken back to her house. For me, this was further proof that I wasn't alone, that someone cared.

Now God began to speak to me personally through His word. What a thrill this was. Who can describe it? The words just leapt out of a book as I read them. 'Leave Me to open and close doors!'

A few days later, I was taken back to the motel. I lounged in the sun, as though I hadn't a care in the world. There I met a lovely schoolteacher and her elderly mother who were staying there for a week or so. They listened to my story, and then invited me to share evening meals with them during their stay. I was given so much food I couldn't eat it all. I sat each evening at their table like a Queen. Food that was left over was given to me for my breakfast and lunch. No problem, I had a fridge at my disposal. Later, it was through this good lady that I was to find my next post with another family. When their stay at the motel came to an end, they gave me all the leftovers. Not twelve baskets full, but a fridge full, bursting to capacity. Who says the 'good measure' isn't pressed down, shaken together and running over. When I finally left to start work with my second family, I left the fridge half full. Was someone else being sent there, to learn the same lesson of trust and provision that I was starting to learn? While saying goodbye to these lovely people, something was pressed into my hand; a ten dollar note.

So I had passed through another groove on the Turntable and in it, I had become aware of God's wonderful keeping power; being kept by the power of God. The central pivot holding my record firmly in place, and around which I was rotating, was the desire to 'keep that which I had committed to Him!' And what had I committed to Him? My whole life!

The second family, the Greens, reimbursed the first for my airfare but I was still in debt. Once a week I went to a neighbour to do housework and was able to earn a little pocket money but I took nothing from the family until I was out of debt, and that took some months. There were four children to care for, piles of washing and piles of ironing each day. Everything was just dropped on the floor after use. A bath towel was meant to be used only once, even if it had only wiped a pair of hands. I did a very naughty thing to save the everlasting unnecessary washing in the machine: I picked up the bath or hand towels from the floor, folded them beautifully, and then placed them back in the airing cupboard. No one was suspicious, and no one was harmed as a result. But there were a lot of things where I drew the line; when all the work fell on me. After all, I am only one rather small person. I remember one drastic mistake I made with the dishwasher. I had never used all these mechanical things before and found them quite confusing at first. Mrs Green had some striped cereal bowls, I suppose made from plastic; they certainly weren't china. I put them in the dishwasher with all the rest of the items. But the temperature was wrong; far too hot, so when I took them out they had become every shape imaginable. If they hadn't looked so funny, I would have felt far worse about it. They all found their way into the garbage can. Another mishap was putting a red towel in with white underwear; to save time of course. The underwear came out the most exquisite pink, so beautifully and evenly dyed; and each time I was forgiven.

There was no order of the day. I knew what had to be done, and was allowed to do it my way. There was a huge plastic swimming pool in the garden and I often stayed in it quite a while to cool off from the extreme summer heat and humidity. Houses had air-conditioning; otherwise all windows and doors had wire mesh fittings to keep out the bugs when they were open. The mesh screens made me feel shut in and certainly reduced the light inside but, then, lights were left on all day.

I had a proper day off, and took many trips around the area including New York City. I missed going to church very much and, as I always had to work on Sundays, I took a subway train on my days off to downtown New York where I could take Holy Communion. I did my best to like the city, but I couldn't stand the noise, the rush and the summer heat. I stayed permanently wet, with clothes sticking to my body. The lavish stores, well air-conditioned, were so vast, I got lost in them but at least I could dry off inside them. Manholes in the roads belched steam from the subways. After one experience on the subway involving a filthy-minded man, I refused to venture on them again so that was the end of my weekly communion. I had been warned about this kind of experience but it is different in reality, especially on a crowded subway train where there is no chance of moving away. I was seldom able to walk far without some hanger-on trying to get acquainted. My response was to ignore them and after a while I realised they had gone. I found it all rather nauseating.

I found no joy in the city. Museums were interesting but that was about all. Not even central park aroused any enthusiasm. There were altogether too many people and far too much noise. As the weeks progressed, I found a smaller town I preferred to visit, White Plains, which would later become my home for a while.

But how I loved the winters; by Christmas, snow lay thick on the ground and temperatures went well below freezing, then the thrill of spring as the first blades of grass appeared in a world that had been white for so long.

At last the fare from England was paid off, and I had saved enough money to make a long-awaited trip to California to see my eldest sister (Monica). By now I had bought myself a bicycle. I also bought my first camera from a New York store; thus I began keeping a record of all my movements on slides as well as writing accounts of them. For some reason at the store, the salesman asked for my name. 'Wride,' I said. When I'd spelt it out slowly, which I always have to do, he turned to me and said, 'I knew a man by that name during the war, when I was stationed at Winchester, Hampshire.' It turned out to be my father!

I booked a seat on a Trailways bus, leaving New York City for San Diego, California, with two suitcases and an awful cold! The bicycle came too.

From my diary – 8 April 1963

'At 3.45 pm, I left New York for San Diego. The bus was packed. I had a terrible cold with bouts of coughing which I couldn't stop, owing to a tickle in my throat - most embarrassing. We drove through heavy showers, arriving at Philadelphia at 7.45 pm. The city lights looked beautiful; reflected in the river. 2 am: we drove into Pittsburgh. It was very cold. 4.45 am: the dawn appeared and at 6 am, we reached Cleveland, Ohio. By now, sleep had almost overtaken me but I forced myself to keep awake as I might never pass this way again. I had to keep awake. We now started to cross the Great Plains, reaching Toledo on Lake Erie at 8.45 am. The scenery reminded me of England, only on a gigantic scale. Huge fields with colts and pigs in them. Small lakes with communities built around them. 12.15 noon we reached Illinois. I could see the skyline of smoky Chicago in the distance. 3 pm: Left Chicago. Saw telegraph wires for the first time since I'd left England. 5.30 pm: Mendota, small and lovely. Doves were cooing. 2.30 am: Wednesday, Des Moines. 5.45 am: Iowa. The trees were in full bloom and looked beautiful. 6 am: Omaha, Nebraska. I had bacon, eggs, toast and coffee for breakfast. 8.45 am: we left Omaha. The fields are like patchwork quilts, black and white cattle standing against a background of green, giving a chessboard effect. 9.30 am: Lincoln, Nebraska. 12.15 noon: Hastings.

'The air is noticeably softer. Left at 1.15 pm. Saw a cock pheasant. We passed through some very heavy storms. 5.30 pm: Wray, Colorado. 6.15 pm: lovely sunset over the plains, casting a glow

> over the patchwork quilted fields. 9.50 pm: Denver Colorado, standing a mile high.
>
> 'Here I decided to make a stop. I hadn't washed in three days, and had not slept much either. My cold had miraculously vanished, but my legs were swollen to double their normal size. When I got out of the bus and stood on my legs they felt heavier than lead, and I had a feeling they wanted to burst out of their skins. Finding a very third rate hotel, I washed and lay down, first seeing the door was locked. Even so, I didn't feel safe but was too exhausted to worry. I just had to sleep and get my poor swollen legs back to normal.
>
> 'The next day, feeling refreshed and so much better, and my legs only half the size, I decided to go on a sight-seeing bus tour in the evening. It turned out to be another 65 miles drive, or thereabouts. We visited Denver's amphitheatre which seated 10,500 people. The scenery was dry and barren. I took slides of Red Rock, Titanic, and Creation. We were shown dinosaur marks found in the rocks and where in 1936 bones had been discovered which were now in Denver Museum. Buffalo Bill's Ranch was also included on the tour. Returning to the same hotel I slept soundly. Next day my legs were back to their normal size.'

On all my travels I carried an electric element for heating water and a small enamel pot to boil water in. One can travel all over the United States using the same small two-pin plugs throughout – most convenient. I also had with me packets of tea, coffee, sugar, and a jar of dried milk. This greatly reduced my food costs as I could drink whenever I liked in my hotel rooms. I ate one good meal a day with perhaps a sandwich or just an apple at midday.

At that time, and no doubt still today, one could buy a bus ticket covering a certain period, enabling one to break the journeys, and then pick up the bus later in the week. I had always wanted to see Colorado, so that was the reason I'd made a short stopover. I enjoyed eating at McDonald's, although I found the decor rather gaudy, the food was excellent!

On Saturday at 4.30 pm, I caught a bus from Denver to start on the last lap of my journey. I was feeling fine again and wanted to get on with it. Oh, the thrill of seeing the Rockies, and with snow on them. It's one thing studying everything with a map and photos but to be there in person, absorbing the atmosphere, is something quite different.

From my diary:

'The winding road led us up and up to 11,000 ft. Snow lay everywhere and it was so cold. 8 pm: we had supper in Vail, a ski resort. I was fascinated to see bathers swimming outside in a steaming pool. 4.15 am: Sunday, we crossed the boarder into Utah. 6.55 am: we reached Salt Lake City on Easter Day - Hallelujah! But I didn't join the Mormons for a service. I only changed over to a Greyhound bus for Las Vegas.'

(My diary records a 'frightful' journey, but no details about it.)

'Now we started to cross desert land with clouds of dust blowing up behind us as we raced along. Enormous cacti all over the place, but there were no flowers to be seen. How I would love to see a desert in full bloom after the rains. 6.30 pm: we finally reached Las Vegas where I planned to make another stop. I couldn't miss seeing a bit of this infamous place. I took a taxi to a recommended hotel, although the driver wasn't slow in telling me there were 'different hotels if you wish!' I was quick to let him know I 'didn't wish.'

'After a meal, I went sightseeing. What a place; an oasis in the desert all right but what an oasis. I only dared to peep inside the open doors of the gambling houses. Neon signs flashed everywhere, some tuning in circles, advertising every type of thing imaginable. I rose early next morning to see the town again. I suppose everyone had been gambling all night as, except that the neon lights were out, it appeared just as I had left it the previous evening. Actually, I found the atmosphere rather frightening.

'On Monday at 9.50 am, I changed back to a Trailways bus. This time I had a companion, an elderly ex-boxer wearing a ten gallon hat. He proved most interesting, pointing out the sights and telling me the history of the places as we went. He always helped me in and out of the bus and each time he took my elbow, and I almost screamed with pain; his grip was so strong, I thought my bones would break. As there were now only a few passengers, I was able to stretch myself out on a seat and get some sleep.

'At 12.30 noon, we crossed the border into California. There was a fruit inspection. Men boarded the bus to inquire if we had any fruit. One person had an apple and it was taken away. There were very strict rules about what was allowed over the border, them being a safety measure against diseases. The bus was also sprayed before we were allowed to move on. 12.45 pm: we drove into the Sierra Nevadas, one could see the Los Angeles smog lying in the valley. 8.30 pm: San Diego! There was my sister waiting to greet me, and was I tired: 3,421 miles in eight days!'

One of the first things that struck me soon after my arrival in California was how all types of flowers were blooming together. In England, we had learned that flowers bloomed at different seasons, but here no such law seemed to exist.

My immediate reaction was that it was wrong. From this I learned a great lesson in life. Because things are different from what we are accustomed to do not necessarily mean they are wrong or, for that matter, we are right. How careful we have to be when we think our way is the only right and proper way, and our interpretation of God's Word is the only right one and want everyone to agree and walk as we think they should. True, the Lord may have convicted one heart that this or that is wrong but that does not give us the liberty to insist that, because that way or that thing is wrong for us, it must therefore be wrong for someone else. What conceit to think that the Lord has only given us the right interpretation and no one else. After a while we adjust to the new and unfamiliar and, were we to return to our first way of life, we would find that what was old and familiar to us then has now become new and unfamiliar again. There seems to be a constant need for readjustment which is never easy.

My sister, Monica, had a bungalow on 3rd Avenue. Up the steps to the entrance she had lots of potted plants. A hibiscus was in one. One day as I sat there in the sun, a beautiful humming bird hovered over a flower, sucking the nectar. Its wings were invisible to my eyes. It was only about a foot away. Not far from the bungalow a foot-bridge spanned a large ravine. I would scramble to the bottom where, in the intense heat, I picked fruits like loganberries which were growing wild; then, grappling clumps of grass as hand-holds, I'd pull myself up to the top again. The fruit tasted marvellous. I think that ravine is now a major road. What a terrible noise there must be after the peace and quiet that once reigned there.

Outside Monica's bungalow in San Diego

On May Day, friends from Chula Vista took us to Tijuana and Tecate in Mexico. We watched a parade with bands playing, and a placid donkey that stood with a cart decorated all over with sombreros. I wanted to take a slide of them but not buy one. The owner badgered me every time I focused my camera. He would not get out of the way. Eventually I got a photo when he turned his back.

1st Avenue, San Diego - 1963

My bicycle arrived from New York. Oh, the bikes I've bought and sold. This one, however, became well travelled. It even returned with me to England where it was used until it fell to pieces.

My favourite place in San Diego was Balboa Park with its magnificently ornate Spanish style buildings set amid gum trees, gracefully arched walls with bougainvillea, in purple and red, draping over the top; vast beds of blazing marigolds, their faces towards the sun; mosaic patios, with ferns, fountains and palms, and seats with blue umbrellas. There were huge ponds filled with enormous goldfish. At one end the botanical garden stood under glass, reflected in almost still water. There were water lilies, looking like wax, floating on clumps of saucer-like leaves. After ten o'clock it was far too hot to remain long in the sunshine.

I now needed work again so on 13 May I took a coach to La Jolla. Finding a room in the International House, I took a job in a motel, cleaning out the rooms. The work proved much more than I could physically manage, so I soon left.

My next job was washing up in a restaurant. This also nearly killed me. After washing up plates, I stacked them in metal baskets which were let down by hand into huge sinks of near-boiling or boiling water. Letting them down wasn't too difficult, but heaving them up and out of the water was a different story. Needless to say, I didn't stay too long at that job either.

Just one little story I remember well from that experience; the person who had recently left, had not left things very clean, so I tried to do a bit of extra cleaning when I had time. One day, an inspector came to inspect the area but it did not meet with his approval. He started blasting me as though I was to blame. I was quick to inform him I'd just started and it wasn't my dirt or my fault. For some reason, he took my name and address and asked my age. When I told him, he all but accused me of lying. Without a word I fetched my passport and showed it to him. He looked quite amazed then eased up. 'Now you can apologise', I said in a horrible la-de-da British voice. He did.

La Jolla didn't please me as, not being interested in the sea or swimming, there was little else for me. But I quite enjoyed sitting on the cliffs on occasions, watching the emerald green sea rolling in and out. I began to notice that after about six waves, the seventh was much longer and came much further up the sandy beach. A couple, well in from the water's edge, were lying down with a radio on, basking in the sun. The tide was coming in. I counted the waves as they rolled in and yes, every seventh seemed to roll further up the beach. Knowing what would finally happen, I sat wide-eyed on the cliff and waited. It was only a matter of time when I counted ... five, six, seven. I watched this long gentle wave roll further and further up the beach as though it had an engine behind it; slowly it rolled clean under the couple who were lying there. They sat up with a start but it was too late. They were soaked. I grinned from my observation seat, high and dry.

After two months, I returned to San Diego. There was no work to be found except heavy work which I just couldn't manage. My 35th birthday was celebrated with a photo of me sitting by an exotic bloom, and an evening meal out somewhere with my sister.

I had planned to move on to San Francisco which everyone said I had to visit. So at 4 am the next morning I set off by bus, arriving at 6.40 pm and taking a room at the YMCA. Work was impossible to find. Then quite suddenly, the urge came upon me to learn to type. So, buying a portable typewriter and a teach-yourself typing book, I set about mastering the art of touch typing. Each morning in my room I worked for a few hours as if I were at school. Later, I went sightseeing.

I loved San Francisco. It was so cosmopolitan; so many nationalities, all living together in harmony. I went into Union Square to feed the dozens of pigeons that sat on my arms and head, taking bread out of my hands and sometimes leaving their 'card' behind. I took a ride on that wonderful street car along Powel Street to the terminal. There it was turned around on a turntable, then headed back down the hill again. Chinatown was also explored. It looked lovely at night with all the street signs lit up.

Another time, I walked across the Golden Gate Bridge. It took me forty-five minutes each way. Sadly the mist never cleared all day so I wasn't able to see the top of it.

My room, on the thirteenth floor, commanded a very extensive view over roof-tops. Americans don't seem to be so fussy about pulling curtains at night and I had already followed in the habit. Just because I had a light on didn't mean I had to draw the drapes or, in my case, the shade. I was standing by the window one evening in my slip and bra, gazing out over the amazing jumble of roof-tops when I spied what looked like an almost hidden pair of binoculars pointed in my direction. Concentrating hard, I stared until I felt sure they were focused on me in my half naked state. Then, when I felt there was no doubt at all, I gave the onlooker a smile and a wave and pulled the shade down very slowly. I've often wondered what he, or she, thought. Of course, there were twelve other windows below mine.

There was noise in the Y almost all night long, mostly from doors banging as the occupants returned at all hours. Not being the best of sleepers, especially changing beds so often, I decided to buy some earplugs; at least they shut out the bulk of the noise enabling me to get to sleep. Now, I always travel with a pair handy.

One morning, as I sat typing in my room, I became aware I was being told to move on again; but where to? So often I'm told to do something but never told the details which usually come through obedience by making the move in faith. So I dallied for a day or so. In my heart I knew I had to return to New York. The problem was I had vowed never to return there. I should have guessed. On God's Turntable we are not consulted as to whether we would like to go somewhere and do something; we are expected to be willing to obey at all costs. The Lord never forces us to make the final decision but just waits patiently until we decide. If we obey, we are greatly blessed but if we don't obey, and choose to go our own way, we are courting disaster. I had already reached the stage in my Christian walk where I feared stepping into the wrong groove at the wrong time. I also had learned that disobedience takes us out from the Lord's protection. If we are not in the Way, how can we expect to be in His will? He is the Way and we are told to 'walk ye in it.' Little wonder He puts pressure on us at times to keep us in His way. He knows that out of His way we are very vulnerable, exposed to all the evil around us.

So the pressure was put on me those few days and I hesitated to obey. I knew what I had to do. The self in me didn't want to do it. Soon, however, the guilt of my inactions became too heavy to carry, so I booked a flight for 7 August to return to the place I didn't want to return to. With two suitcases and now a typewriter, I found I needed another hand. As is my wont, I arrived at the airport well on time; I'd rather wait one hour than rush.

I really cannot explain how it happened that, although I was at San Francisco Airport ages before necessary, I still managed to miss my flight. Actually it was quite simple, the sort of thing anyone like me could have done. It was this kind of switched-off thing that used to happen to me at school. I had parted company with both suitcases but carried my typewriter. The flight number was called and I seemed to walk miles to get to the departure gate. There I stood with a crowd of people at the top of a ramp over which was written in English: Only Passengers Beyond this Point. I stared and stared at those words as though they had no meaning. Nothing registered. I was obviously having one of my very switched off spells. I came to when I saw the plane taxiing out. Suddenly I realised I should have been on it, not staring at it. What an idiot I was, I thought, not even capable of boarding an aircraft or understanding plain English. At the top of the ramp, the well wishers began to wave as the plane went further and further away. Not wanting to be conspicuous, I did the same; waving frantically I cried 'bon voyage' to my fast disappearing suitcases on their way to New York.

Making my way back to the check-out, now to become my check-in, I began to explain what had happened to the only pair of ears that happened to be there. The counter was so high, I felt sure the ears could only see my head and nose and with luck my lips moving. When I'd finished my incredible story, the ears asked, 'are you English?' At that precise moment I was sorry even any part of my head was showing. So embarrassed was I that I wanted to drop into the bowels of the earth. What else could I have been with an accent such as mine? I was transferred to another airline and I managed to board without incident. We took wings at 10 am, the flight to Idlewild Airport lasting five hours after which I was finally reunited with my two suitcases.

So what now Lord? On the assurance that 'the Way will open as you go, I was back in New York but didn't know where to turn. I was not in the least bit happy to be back in New York. Only one thought came to my mind and of course, looking back, that was the right thought, leading me on to the next step. I decided to phone a friend I knew.

So stepping into a phone box, I phoned this friend. I'm sure she thought I was mad and incapable of ordering my own life. But I wasn't ordering my own life, the Lord was. How on earth did I know where I was going, and what I was doing, until I received my instructions from my Guide?

How easy it is when you know where you're going. I seldom did, until the door opened after I had arrived. God's guidance can be very vague and seemingly very muddling. It is usually in this apparent muddle that you find His hand is leading you through. He used my friend to do His leading but I doubt if she was even aware of it. How close He must stand to us at times, without our having the slightest knowledge or awareness that He is using us in His will. I had barely finished talking when my money ran out and I had the embarrassing moment of the bell, placed on top of the phone box, ringing with a vengeance announcing to the world that the caller inside had run out of money.

My friend, if she still was my friend, picked me up and took me back to her house. I'm sure she had only one thought in her mind, and that was to bundle me back to England by ship. But there was neither ship nor berth on the Turntable at that immediate moment and, as we only travelled on British ships in those days, I couldn't be bundled anywhere. I recognised the Lord was still having His way in spite of my friend's efforts to get rid of me in haste. Next day, however, the 'zeal of the Lord was upon her' again. This time, I was whisked off to a huge departmental store in White Plains and given an interview. Another miracle: I was accepted. My friend, to put it mildly, was overjoyed.

Three days of training upstairs, then we were on the floor. All mistakes should have been left upstairs but mine came down with me and remained on the floor for some weeks to follow. Everything was so complicated. We had duplicate triplicates, or was it triplicate duplicates? How was it I managed to get the carbon paper back to front underneath, so that what should have been on the triplicate appeared on the reverse side of the duplicate? No one else seemed to have this problem.

Then there was the inevitable question: 'Will this be charge or cash?' What a stupid question. Of course everything was charge and our cash register was festooned with names and addresses of customers who never paid their bills, and on no account were we to let them run up another account. I mean, how could you ask a customer if she would mind waiting while you checked the blacklist to see if her name was on it? The list grew larger and longer as the months progressed; no way could I memorise the list of forbidden names. So in went the charge card into the machine but often, as I pressed down on the lever, only half the address and name appeared on the bill. Somehow I couldn't have put it in straight. I learned more of the inside workings of the cash register than the outside. I would press the wrong keys for the wrong departments, ending up with ladies hats on men's underwear, or children's toys on ladies shoes. Only a desperate phone call to the floor manager could rectify the mistake. 'I'm so sorry,' I used to say, trying not to laugh at my capability of doing even the simplest of things back to front. The poor man must have worn out a pair of shoes in the first week I was on the floor.

Apparently I posed quite a problem. I laughed too much and got on far too well with the other sales personnel. The idea was that the more people who hated each other the more they fought for sales. I was moved around from department to department but still got on with everybody. How I was never sacked I'll never know. Anyway, I gave them my British best, even if at the end of the day my total takings were well below average. I was used to being on the bottom rung anyway.

Now I had to find a room to live in close to the store. Not earning much, I knew I wouldn't find much. Eventually, I found one within walking distance. There were two of us, a Polish lady in one room, and me in the other. We shared the kitchen, bathroom and toilet. The owner, from foreign parts, showed me to my room. Leaving my cases there, I was taken to the kitchen. 'At no time are you boz to be in zee kitchen togezer,' I was told. I've forgotten why. 'Mrs Balzac, she come back at such and such a time. She go in and cook meal – yes? After Mrs Balzac finish – yes, you go in.'

What could Mrs Balzac be like, I thought. Ah well, knowing me, I can guess what will happen - and it did. I got to like Mrs Balzac. She was interesting, coming from Europe, and had much to talk about that interested me. Soon we were even daring to chat together in the kitchen.

I began to notice my things were moved about in my room. This annoyed me but I said nothing as, until I could find another room, this one had to suffice. One evening, some time later, Mrs Balzac and I prepared our evening meal together in the kitchen. I always ate a good midday meal at the store, they were very good and at a reasonable cost, so I didn't bother much in the evening. Mrs Balzac cooked her meal and sat down to eat it. I also sat down with her at the table with my meal. We were so engrossed in conversation that neither of us heard the footfall on the stairs. Suddenly the kitchen door was pushed open and our landlady, from foreign parts, burst in upon us like some bird of prey seeking whom she might devour. 'I tought I make it clear zat at no time are you boz to ...'

Rising quickly from my seat, I faced our uninvited guest who filled the doorway with her girth. 'We are not children,' I said calmly, and with all the dignity I could muster at just five feet tall. 'If we choose to eat together, we choose to eat together - yes?' Feeling the flush of victory, I returned to the kitchen table, and continued our conversation as if nothing had happened. A slight rush of air about me told me our landlady from 'foreign parts' had silently departed. Mrs Balzac and I enjoyed quite a few meals 'togezer' until I found another room.

I can hardly say I grew in grace and favour as a saleswoman at the store. I was a bit of a curiosity to the customers who sat and chatted to me as if I had opened a psychiatric letting-off-steam department. I became involved with all their private problems with husbands and children which, while I was not unprepared to listen to, was hardly the reason why I was there. However, I soon discovered that if I hovered around with an air of intelligence, plus an item in my hand, it looked as if I were selling it. But I didn't get away with it. My takings at the end of the day were too poor for their liking. The problem was there was no aggression among us. Loving your neighbour as yourself didn't come into it. What they wanted was competition, and hating your neighbour was far more likely to give them the total takings they were looking for at the end of each day. Aggressive salesmanship was what was needed to bring the figures up to the grand totals that brought smiles all around. Actually, I hated selling, not my neighbour. I couldn't get any interest in what I was selling so I took myself off into the stock room and kept that well in order, eventually knowing exactly what was there, what was sold, and what should be ordered. I took great pains to explain this to the area manager, or manageress, who visited each department now and then, no doubt to see individual's weekly totals. As I explained, 'The success of our department is due wholly to the excellent organisation in the stock room; no stock, no sales!' I was kept on.

By now, I was looking hard for another room. I refused to stay where I was with all my things being shifted about each day but with money in short supply I didn't expect to find much. Someone gave me a lead. The house was of doubtful character; of that there was no doubt. It was dirty, full of dubious characters, male and female, who clearly had been gathered off the streets.

The room I rented was reasonably large, but filthy. Saying my prayers on the first night, I slid into very questionable bed linen that had been provided. Next day after work I set to work cleaning the room, buying bed linen and three floor mats. The room became home to me for many months. Later, I discovered another woman who worked at the store had a room on the top floor. We became friends.

In its day, the house must have been beautiful, lived in by wealthy people. Up a flight of wooden steps, leading to a double fronted front door, there was a wooden balcony running the whole length of the house. The hall was spacious, with a wide staircase, leading to the first floor. The large landing led off to big rooms. There were two bathrooms. One I kept clean as I used it, the other was filthy, with empty beer cans and liquor bottles hidden behind curtains hanging over an empty book shelf.

Having no kitchen, I bought very little food, as there was nowhere to keep it. Still, I ate a good meal at the store so didn't want much in the evenings. I stood my milk bottle in the wash basin in my room, almost submerged in water, in the hope of keeping it cool; what a hope when the temperatures were over 90° F. With my element and enamel pot, I was always able to have a drink.

In winter, however, things were much easier. The screens we fixed in the open windows in summer to keep out the bugs were now, in winter, held in place on the outside of the very wide window ledge. This became my fridge and an excellent one it was. In sub-zero temperatures, I became an expert in knowing just how long I could leave my milk outside before the cream froze on the top, lifting the metal cap. Sometimes I miscalculated and found the cream had risen up about an inch above the top, with the cap still on it. Actually, I found it all rather fun, despite the hardship. Having everything so easy and comfortable can be frightfully boring. Roughing it has always brought me a lot of pleasure.

In April 1964, after eight months at the store, the pace began to catch up with me. My headaches were more frequent and the noise incessant. There were no windows on the floor and the constant feeling of being shut in under fluorescent lighting began to get me down. At the rate I was going, I could never find a decent room and the dirt and atmosphere of that house where I lived was also taking its toll on me. So I decided: I would sail for England for a while. My American visa allowed me to stay out of the country for 364 days. If I didn't return within the year I would have to reapply for entry. Surely I would know or receive clear guidance as to what I should do within that space of time?

This time there was a British ship on the Turntable - The Queen Elizabeth, so I booked a berth, sailing to England on 2 April 1964. Why did I sail? Just to have the experience - no more and I hope never again; the reason being that I was permanently giddy during the journey. I was told it was a form of seasickness. On deck outside I was all right, but it was far too cold to stay out there all day. The entertainment didn't interest me either. So I endured five days, I think it was, of boredom and giddiness. The only sight worth remembering was passing another ship at night. It truly was a wonderful sight.

Everyone got excited when the English coast came into view. It was fun watching it grow bigger and bigger. Finally we docked at Southampton where Mummy was waiting to meet me. The ship looked enormous in dock but at sea I had no feeling of its size.

The next four months was a time when I didn't know which way to turn. The door stood open for me to return to the United States, or to remain in England. I wanted neither.

Looking back, though, I realise that through experience there are many times when we are asked and expected to sit still, and see how the matter will turn. A boat going into a lock has to wait until the water has lifted it onto a higher level before it is released. It is literally held there. It cannot and dare not move. We come again to God's timing. Except for these periods of waiting, the dove-tailing of His plans in my case could never have taken place with the unbelievable precision I now know is so possible with Him. The 'full stop ahead,' should be growing time in the Spirit. Perhaps He has something extra special to say to us which we will only hear if we are absolutely still.

The voice of the Spirit comes very softly to each heart and we won't hear it if we are not in close communion with the Lord. The rush of the world deafens us so often to this still small voice and I believe that, if we really tell the Lord we want to hear Him, He will - if necessary - bring us to a halt so that this communion with Him may be perfected. If other voices are not checked, we will fail to hear His. When His will becomes our will and His desires our desires, then we hear His voice, and guidance becomes real. I have also learned never to act if there is any element of doubt in my heart. The next move will always be presented by absolute assurance. You may not hear His voice each time but nevertheless you will know it to be the promptings of the Spirit.

Not knowing what to do on my return to England, I decided to visit our old home in Winchester. I was keen to revisit old haunts. There was indeed a great change. The part of the garden (at Beaconsfield House) where we had laboured so hard to make our tennis court now had two houses on it. The conservatory where 'Clean All Tools' had been written on the wall, and where I thought I could still taste and smell those watercress sandwiches, had also gone. The only sign remaining that the conservatory had once been there was a few white-washed bricks indicating the outline where the frame had been. I remembered how one of our rabbits, which we let lose in there, accidentally jumped into the water butt where we cleaned the tools, and drowned.

A large area of the copse that bordered the drive had gone when the corner on which it stood had been curved, making it less dangerous for motorists. The stables, harness room and garage still remained.

I went through the front door, explaining who I was. The house had been converted to offices. When I told people how long we had lived there, I was taken around on a tour. Oh, how the memories flooded back, and how interested they were to hear about them. Our one bathroom had been divided and made into two toilets. The enormous airing cupboard with its huge water tank, which Daddy had installed, was still there. Up in the attic the old wallpaper hung down in parts and I remembered Grandma's hip bath that used to stand there. Nothing had really changed except the dividing wall between the dining-room and drawing-room had been pulled down to make a conference room. The black marble and wooded mantelpieces were still as they used to be. I pictured the Sevres that had stood at each end of them, with a chiming clock in the centre of each, but couldn't remember what had become of them.

Much of the garden had gone where the two houses now stood, including my secret hideout under the cherry tree. The old water butt outside was still full with murky mucky water and, no doubt, gnat larvae. Yes, it brought both happy and sad memories with it, but I was glad to have made the visit. We cannot hold time still, neither do I want to, but whenever I think of our old home it is always as it was when I was a child, not how I saw it in later life.

I also visited the convalescent home in Bournemouth where I was put through the mill. The grinding had been very thorough in that place, preparing me for much rougher and tougher assignments which no doubt, unknown to me at that time, made some of the following events smoother because of it. Now I see that had I not been so dealt with in that place, I would never have had the self-discipline to get through much that was to come.

Hebrews 12: 11 says: 'No discipline seems pleasant at the time, but painful. Later on, however, it produces a harvest of righteousness and peace for those who have been trained by it.' NIV Bible.

Years later I was able to say, 'Thank you Lord. You did it because You loved me!'

Chapter 6

It was three months before I felt an inner pressure to return to the United States. How does one explain that one is waiting for 'guidance,' especially to a person who hasn't a clue what you are talking about, or had any experience in such matters? It all must sound quite absurd. My promising career had gone to the wind on some ridiculous pretext of 'doors being shut' and now I was wandering around, not knowing where I was going next. Why didn't I settle down with a steady job, get a decent home?

'Find yourself a man' was repeated advice thrown at me. How did they know I hadn't already found a man I would dearly settle with - but he was not available? Just because I didn't share my personal life with anyone, didn't mean I hadn't wanted these things. It was always my will against His will. Whose will was I going to follow? Herein lay the constant battle; Thy will be done, not mine. So I had to keep following, following, following, wherever I was led, regardless of what people thought or said. I had stepped onto God's Turntable which just kept me moving along with it. Never would I have chosen this way of life, whose work I was called to do; learning to live in constant earthly uncertainly; until my security was firmly planted and established in the Lord. Only He knew what He was doing, whose life He was touching. I seldom did, but go on with Him I had to; there was no turning back.

The more I knew with complete certainty that I walked and moved under God's guidance, the more I prayed to be able to accept whatever it involved, the more I was able to accept it, the more wonderful the revelations became; the great coincidences that could never have been by chance, the perfect timings that had been calculated to the minute, to the exact day. No, in spite of what everyone might have said, I knew my Guide and the more I knew Him, the less I wanted to step off that well-timed Turntable. There was an excitement and buoyancy that had begun to take place in this guidance, in spite of the hardships and sacrifices. I was still prepared to go on whatever the cost.

I couldn't get over the store in New York saying they would reemploy me if ever I returned to the United States. It was certainly not on my prowess as a sales woman. On my arrival in White Plains, New York, I was greeted enthusiastically by those I knew. The lost sheep had returned. Ah, but what had the lost sheep returned to; the same pitiable financial state, the same dirty house?

'How lovely to see you again; I'm afraid I don't have the same room, only a smaller one.'

'But it's only half a room.'

'Yes, it was a large room that has been divided into two. You stay?'

'Yes, I'll stay.' Oh Lord, I suppose one day I shall have enough money to live in a nice clean place again. At least I was now next to the bathroom I used to keep clean.

'Why, bless my soul. Oh, 'tis good to see yer again' an old toothless Irish woman grinned at me as I started to clean the bathroom again. Ah well, I thought, at least I'm welcome everywhere.

My half residence was very small; I could touch the dressing table while I sat up in bed. Obviously my section was the end of a once lovely big room, as there was an enormous bay window almost the width of it. During the winter, I fed a grey squirrel that leapt off the overhanging branches of a tree and ate what I gave it on the window sill.

All went well for about six months. My tiny abode was almost home. The other half of the room hadn't been occupied. Then one night I heard a new occupier come in on the other side of the thin partition. Obviously he was worse for drink. When eventually he staggered into bed, he moaned, snorted, talked, shouted, and cleared his throat in a manner that made me almost sick. I knew I would have to start searching for another room. Also my warning light had reappeared; headaches. I realised the pressure and pace at the store, and life in general was getting on top of me. There was constant noise everywhere, even at night. I was moving faster and faster and couldn't stop. My laughter had become a bit hysterical, and sleep did not come so easily. Something had to change somewhere.

I was barely in a position to leave my job before I found another. How would I live in the meantime? New York was hardly a place to be out of work with nowhere to live. Did I have the faith to burn my boats behind me? Had I not already proved God's providence? Could I believe strongly enough in Him that He would provide for me, even if I left one job before I found another? Was I prepared to risk my all on Him? Was the amount of faith I already had enough to take such a step? But quite unknown to me, events were already leading me to a situation that forced me to take that step in faith to prove that He could and would provide yet again for me in my extremity.

On my return to the United States, I had joined an Episcopalian Church close to where I lived. I sang in the choir and attended regularly. One day I was asked by a lady I knew only by sight if I would like to help her prepare a meal for the men's Quiet Evening that was shortly to take place. I agreed. Later, while we sat having a meal together, I told her my story and how I should have to look for other work. She was a social worker and understood my position perfectly. The evening came to a close and I never gave the conversation another thought.

Also on my return to New York I'd felt pressure to go to a typing school. I had worked hard at my teach-yourself typing book and had become quite a good touch typist but didn't have much, if any, idea how to set things out on paper. I registered with Teffts Typing School. There were thirty pupils in my class, all typing hell for leather at the same time on thirty typewriters of all makes, shapes and sizes (as were the pupils). How I didn't go mental with all that noise I'll never know. I returned home in the evenings with a pounding headache that by now only tablets could relieve. But good news was on the way, so I thought. Someone told me of a nice clean room that was available just a few doors away on the same street from the dirty house I lived in. It was indeed clean; so clean in fact, that one could barely move for fear of making a mark. Any port in a storm I thought, so accepted it. There were no cooking facilities as usual and, of course, the bathroom and toilet were shared. Quite elated with the accommodation I moved in, carrying all my goods and chattels bit by bit up the street, then upstairs to my new clean room. It took me quite a while but by now I was used to doing everything on my own.

Around three weeks later, I came back from the store exhausted; mentally and physically. I lay flat on my bed trying to relax, too weary to care about anything. My head felt as if there was an iron band around it. I banged it on the bedpost in an attempt to relieve the pain. It had no effect. Suddenly, girls upstairs started thumping and banging around to music right above me. A terrible fear took hold of me at that moment; I had to escape. In my desperation to find rest and peace, I got up and walked out of the house into the street. I had no idea where I was going, or what I intended to do. The pain in my head was now intolerable.

In a daze, I slowly wandered up the tree-lined street until I passed a large house. Quite unexpectedly I heard the still small voice inside me say, 'ring that bell.' The effect was electrifying. All of a sudden, I seemed to be lifted off my feet and carried up the steps to the front door. After ringing the bell, I waited until a very nice middle-aged lady came to the door.

'Do you know of a room for rent?' I asked. 'I'm looking for one.'

'Why yes', she answered, 'I have an attic flat vacant. Would you like to see it?'

It was a lot more expensive but I thought I could just make it on my salary if I were very careful. Anything for some peace and quiet! So, within three weeks of carting my belongings from the first house to the second, I began carting them again from the second house to the third. Finally, when everything was taken to the attic, I was 'all in,' both literally and metaphorically; but peace at last.

Work at the store wasn't going well, however. I was physically tired with being on my feet for hours on end, plus the fact that I seemed to have to do the later shifts up until 10 pm, once a week. I was always the one who had to take the first lunch break at 11 am and, except for a tea break of 10 minutes in the afternoon, I was on my feet until 5.30 pm. Afterwards I walked home. Once again, everything was getting on top of me. One day no one wanted to do the late shift and as usual it fell on me. That meant working from 1 pm to 10 pm. It was the end! I couldn't take any more. I warned the floor manager I wouldn't be in to do it. He didn't believe me but he did when I didn't turn up! The next day without saying a word, I collected my things from my locker at 5.30 pm and walked out for the last time. A mean trick … well perhaps.

Now the fear that I had tried to avoid took hold of me. I was out of a job with no money coming in, a higher rent to pay, plus typing lessons. I shared all this with my very understanding landlady. She didn't seem in the least bit worried.

'You'll find a job my dear. Something will turn up.'

Of that I was sure but what in the meantime? The immediate problem was not money but me. I just had to force myself to relax. I began setting the alarm clock for every 10 minutes, forcing myself to lie flat on the bed or the floor without moving. Every muscle in my body was twitching and it took a lot of willpower to bring them under control. Slowly over the days I lengthened the time of keeping still until finally I felt myself going limp. Only as my body began to flop did the pain in my head lessen in intensity. But now with the limpness came the tears. I couldn't stop them no matter how I tried. I just cried and cried and cried. Very slowly, though, I began to pick myself up and get myself under control. How wrong it is to bottle things up with a proverbial stiff upper lip, when tears have been given us as a means of release. Shedding tears has brought me relief and release so many times during untold heartaches and hardships.

Looking back over this period, God was taking me out into the depths of trust and faith in which, as yet, He hadn't tested me. He was now asking for blind faith from me; such faith that no situation or circumstance could shatter it. There was nothing in sight at that moment but the Lord had me in His sight. Was that going to be sufficient for me? Would I abandon every earthly prop and trust Him, until I let go of my wits, and relied on His wisdom? It's so easy to believe His promises when everything goes smoothly but to be down is a test of faith taken to its limits. I was cornered in order to learn this lesson of absolute faith in the Lord. I was held fast like that boat in the lock. How often I've learned that when the way is blackest, the brightest is just ahead. If I had only known how safe I was in His loving care and hands, it would have banished every doubt and fear and, no doubt, the headaches.

But I had not yet learned. The certainty in uncertainty; His certainty in our uncertainty! How could He teach me, except by putting me through the testing and experience where I was forced to take hold of His resources? They are always there, overflowing, in abundance. The tragedy is; how often do we take hold of them and use them. With no job and only typing school I had to take hold of those resources. I began to relax more as tensions weren't so great. I would trust. I would believe. I would wait. 'Lord, help my unbelief.' It was exactly six weeks when all the pieces of the newly formed jigsaw puzzle fell into place.

'Telephone for you Shirley,' I heard my landlady shout from the hall. Who on earth could be phoning me at this time of the day, I thought, as I sped down the two flights of stairs. 'Hello,' I said picking up the receiver. It was the lady from the church, the one I'd helped at the men's Quiet Evening.

'There's a vacancy as secretary-receptionist at the home where I work. I immediately thought of you. I've told the boss already and he's prepared to see you when you're free.' I was glad to be sitting down; the title terrified me? Could I do it? Was I capable? Doubt began to fill my mind but I determinedly turned out such thoughts. Of course I could do it. Of course I'm free. The interview was fixed for soon afterwards.

Sweating with nerves, I met the boss. He was such a nice kindly man. I faced him with the whole truth and nothing but the truth. He assured me I didn't need qualifications and quite understood if my longhand was faster than my shorthand. Actually my shorthand was non-existent but that had been included in the whole truth. There would be the switchboard to learn immediately but the rest I would be shown. Of course typing would be very necessary.

'You do type, do you Shirley?'

Why, of course I type. Hadn't I started two years ago for this very moment? Within 24 hours I heard I'd been accepted. It was just another Turntable Miracle.

On 24 May 1965, I entered my new office with fear and trembling. Never in my life had I had such a good job as this. One look at the switchboard and I thought I'd never master it. Inner panic was taking over, so I sat down and tried to keep calm. All this was quite ridiculous as, after a few lessons, I found it one of the easiest and most enjoyable parts of the job.

'Good morning, Jennie Clarkson Home. Just one moment please.' Plugs in, keys twiddled, pushed or pulled (nothing was automatic), and the right office connected. Blinking light? Someone needs me. Orange light; someone's hung up. I just loved it. After a while I asked for a proper headpiece that I could sling over my head leaving both hands free to work the switchboard. My knowledge of typing proved quite adequate for the requirements. I also had a lot of organisation to do for social workers, psychiatrists, and for transportation.

Above: The Jennie Clarkson Home in Valhalla,New York where Shirley worked

Left: Shirley typing in her office at the Jennie Clarkson Home. 'The telephone exchange was great fun'

The Jennie Clarkson Home was for dependent and neglected children whose backgrounds were rather sad. They were certainly given every opportunity in the home and various schools to make up for so much they'd never had. But can anything make up for the lack of a good home with love and security?

My front office which I shred with the head housemother had a lovely view over the grounds. The home was air-conditioned against the humid heat of summer and warm during the cold winters. At the entrance hall, coffee burped in a percolator most of the morning; one just went down and helped oneself. The much higher salary easily covered the rent of my attic flat and the next immediate need; a car. Now, I thought, I have to set about finding one. But I need not have worried. There was one waiting for me on the Turntable. In fact I was already in contact with the right person who owned it. I made one good friend at the typing school and it was her husband who had just reconditioned a car and wanted to sell it. It was in excellent condition. A blue Ford Falcon, automatic.

'You must buy it on credit Shirley,' I was informed. 'Or else you won't stand in good stead with the bank and will never get a loan in the future.' I hated that method of buying, as the payments hung over my head for months; but when in Rome one does what Rome does, or does one? I did, until I couldn't stand paying that way any longer, so I settled the balance in one go. Just too bad if I didn't stand in good stead with the bank, I thought.

Shirley and her Ford Falcon: Nov 1965

My British driving licence was not accepted in the United States so I had to get a permit until I passed their driving test. I found it more a test of nerves than driving. An automatic drive is so easy but the traffic; nerve racking. I hurtled around the suburbs, trying to cope with traffic, signs, one-way streets, lanes and the mad onward rush of cars whose horns were loud enough to wake the dead. I thought I was quite a good driver in England but this was something I'd never envisaged. No time to think, just keep moving, traffic and noise without ceasing. At least I didn't have to worry about my feet; they were automatic as well, at least the right one was, the left foot did nothing. But it was never my feet that worried me, it was my head. I finished every driving lesson a mental wreck. On 7 December I finally took my driving test and passed but my nerves never passed; they remained with me permanently every time I drove in the traffic. I couldn't take rush hour so I set off for work much earlier than necessary, and would leave work half an hour later in the evening just to avoid the homeward rush.

My landlady allowed me to put my Falcon round the corner of the driveway at the back of her house. That was fine until the winter came with blizzards and deep snow. The world was transformed into a silent white wonderland. Noise was halved. I had to allow an extra half an hour each morning to dig my way out from the drive to the road which was always kept well swept day and night. Mostly the engine started without trouble. Snow tyres were already on in readiness but even so I went through some hair-raising skids and turns, ending up one evening in a ditch. The snow was so high it had hidden the marked edges of the narrow lane I was driving along and off I shot. The poor old Falcon belched columns of exhaust fumes, in keeping with the burly panting and puffing men who came to my rescue.

The only other indignity I ever suffered was running out of gas on Route 22. I had somehow forgotten to fill up the tank the previous day and couldn't understand why I'd come to a standstill in the middle of a very unsuitable stopping place. Getting out of the car, I started flapping my arms, like a bird trying to get off the ground, trying to attract attention. But no one took the slightest notice of me, so I moved out into the danger zone and continued flapping. Finally a man realised my plight and pulled into the slow lane, stopping further on. Reversing his car, he came to where I had been flapping, and then helped me push the Falcon into the slow lane. He promised to ask the first garage he saw to send out a tow truck. Before long a truck arrived and towed both birds gently along Route 22 back to the garage where it was discovered the Falcon had completely dried up.

In the snowy season, householders were expected to sweep and keep their area of the sidewalk clear and always accessible. I often helped my landlady with a wooden snow shovel and neighbours also came to help.

Every Christmas, I was invited to someone's house for the day; being on my own was never allowed. I thought that was very kind; I always found Americans very generous and friendly people. There were presents galore, and far too much food to consume. TV was the entertainment, not an afternoon walk. One Christmas, everyone thought someone else had invited me for the day but, in fact, no one had. I must admit I felt left out that day. I forget what I ate but later I decided a walk would help pass the time. I crunched my way through the snow, gazing through windows whose curtains were not yet drawn, enjoying the scenes within. When, eventually, people at work found out I had spent the day alone I was in trouble. 'Why didn't you invite yourself?' they said. I couldn't have done. Could you?

For another Christmas I went for a few days with a friend by coach to Allentown, Pennsylvania. The journey was out of this world; the scene was white as far as the eye could see. Every house was decorated with fairy lights, on roofs, and in the trees. There was a full moon which threw ghostly shadows over the fields, and then there were in their millions. Intermittently, great flashes of lightning lit up the landscape as if daytime.

I certainly enjoyed my job, and became most proficient in every way. I also graduated from typing school with 66 wpm. I have a certificate to prove it. I've loved typing ever since, although I never had another job like it again.

In July 1966, I took three weeks holiday in England. I moved around, staying with Mummy and my two sisters (Barbara and Audrey) for a few days at a time. I also visited my last remaining aunt, Connie, at Otterbourne. My other aunt, May, had died in October 1963. The garden was in a terrible mess as no one was there to tend it. It was so cold compared with the heat to which I had now grown accustomed that I got chilblains on my heels. How I missed the sunshine and lovely weather and largeness. In England now, everything struck me as being so small, compact and enclosed. Was I glad to return to 90 deg F and feel warm again!

Not long after I returned to the United States, I felt an inner urge to go to night school to continue learning German. I had taught myself such a lot since that wonderful holiday in Austria in 1959 but now I felt I had to learn conversational German. I registered for adult education classes but learned just as a child learns, by hearing and repetition. At first there was little grammar to study but later I found it necessary to help with tenses etc. It was great fun and mentally most stimulating.

Although I went for a vigorous walk during my lunch hour at work, I was basically sitting down most of the day. Soon I noticed the first signs of middle age spread making headway. A man in the business office and I decided to start jogging around the grounds after work at 5 pm. Little by little, we built up the rounds until I believe we completed 10 in all. On one occasion, we were jogging when a most uncanny rumbling sound developed; it sounded as though huge heavy trolleys on casters were being trundled over a floor in a hollow building.

'A bomb?' asked my friend.

'No', I answered. 'I remember the sound of bombs from the war. This is something else.' Later we learned it had been the tremor of an earthquake somewhere. It certainly had a sound all of its own, not easy to describe.

On 24 July that year, a house mother and I drove to Montreal, Canada, to visit Expo '67. We took her car, also an automatic, taking turns at driving for an hour at a time. A straighter route you couldn't find and, by the time the hour was up, my right foot on the accelerator had all but gone to sleep. The further north we drove the less was the humidity until I felt quite dry; I'd grown used to being permanently damp for roughly three months each year in New York's humid heat.

What I saw of Montreal I liked very much; unfortunately we only had two or three days there. The expo apart, my strongest remembrance was one of the most hair-raising experiences I'd ever known; terrifying. We missed the exit heading south and had to drive miles before reaching the next one which would have put us back on the correct southern route. We were probably averaging around 80 mph when my friend, who thank God was driving, decided to pull off onto the centre road section between the eight lanes of traffic, four in each direction. Reversing the car, we took stock of how we could get back onto the southbound section. We waited until there was a gap in the traffic but we discovered that gaps on main routes don't last very long. Finally an opportunity came and my friend revved up the engine to pull out. But what neither of us had realised was that the ground beneath us was soft, so our get-away was a lot slower than anticipated. By the time the back wheels had cleared the soft ground, the gap in the traffic had closed and we were narrowly missed by an onrushing car that, had it hit us, would have decimated us all. The oncoming car screeched to a halt further up the road; then the driver came and screeched at us. Fortunately the abuse was in French and I didn't understand a word. I was soaked with sweat at the near catastrophe - certainly a close shave with death. Incidents like these did not help my already nervous state every time I drove.

Against everyone's better judgement, I decided I had to see the New York slums. I told a friend I was going, informing her of the train I would be taking and the time I intended to return. 'If I'm not back by 8 pm, please call the police, as I shall carry very little money with me,' I said.

As everyone reckoned I was a 'screwball,' they let me go, shrugging their shoulders as I left. They were right; I would never do such a thing nowadays. I took a train, got off to wherever it was, and started walking. I had no handbag, a thing I seldom carry or even own, and walked as though on business while taking in my surroundings as I went. Never had I seen anything like it.

> *From my diary:*
> 'The buildings are appalling, with lines upon lines of washing slung up between them. Each row of washing drips on the one below and so onto the ground level. Men and women just lounge about, leaning against walls, sitting on the pavements, chatting, chewing, smoking and drinking. Children play in the gutters among the litter, rubbish and beer cans. Now I know what it feels like being the only white person around. A large bundle of laundry comes hurtling out of a high window, narrowly missing me as it falls into the arms of the recipient close by. It is then wheeled off in a shabby old pushchair. I sense desolation and hopelessness everywhere, nothing to live for, nothing to hope for.'

I wandered on until I found it all so nauseating I wanted to get out.

Taking a much earlier train home, my friend was much relieved to see me again; I had survived.

The Fall was one of the most magnificent sights I'd ever seen. Nor far from where I lived was a huge tree that turned yellow and gold, other trees turned crimson; all against the deepest blue skies. The humidity had gone and the crisp autumn air had started to tell us the summer was behind. A girlfriend and I used to go out at weekends in either her car or mine just to gaze at nature's magnificence. At night, when I lay down in bed and closed my eyes, the colours were as vivid as though I was still seeing them during the day. With frosty days, the air was now clear. The trees stood in their last glorious splendour, until a very sharp frost brought the leaves tumbling to the ground, to lie as a carpet fit for kings and queens to walk on. I scuffed through the carpet of so many colours and shades, spreading them before me; it was beautiful but so very short-lived. In no time the trees were bare, with outspread branches waiting to be clad in their white winter drapery.

The centre of my life was the Episcopalian Church. I'd made a lot of friends there and joined in with most activities, as it was close to where I lived. It was always a quiet place where I could retire from the incessant urban noise. Inside, one could listen to glorious silence. Once a week I went into the church to light a candle. I'll explain: when spiritual battles raged and I found the going on the Turntable almost unbearable, I remembered that my life was like that little candle, just a tiny light, lighting up an area of darkness. It helped take away that poor-old-me pity and reminded me I was on a mission, the Lord's mission, to serve Him in the place where He had placed me, whether I liked it or not. I held that little light in my mind's eye and realised how large an area it could light up, if it didn't flicker or waver from the purpose for which it had been set alight. I shall never know how far that flame He lit all those years ago has spread but one thing I do know already; there will be people in heaven because of it.

I also enjoyed wandering through the enormous cemeteries, not because of any inner gloom but simply because they were blissfully silent and uninhabited, on the surface anyway. I walked for hours around one cemetery trying to find my way out, only to arrive back at my starting place. Finally I met someone who rescued me and brought me out among the living again. What monuments man erects to the dead, when One Man has passed through death and resurrection to give us all life!

About two years had elapsed before I had a vague realisation that all was not well in my head again. At first I refused to accept it, believing it would pass. I had a wonderful job with a pension at the end of it, a nice apartment, a car, and plenty of money coming in. What more could I wish for? Surely I wasn't to become unsettled yet again? Why was I always plagued this way? I could take responsibility but not pressure which I suppose comes with it.

The first sign that had been building up was my worsening fear of driving in traffic; the roar and racing on the expressways grew more and more horrific for me. I therefore thought that if I could find somewhere to live in the country, closer to my job, the problem would be solved. It didn't take me long before I found what I thought to be a very pleasant upstairs apartment in quiet surroundings from which I could walk to work each day. It was two years and seven months since I'd wandered along that street in a daze and was told to 'ring that bell.' My landlady was very sorry when I left, although she understood the reason why.

The first problem that I encountered at my new abode was that my new landlady wouldn't give me a receipt for my weekly rent. No way was I going to hand over the said amount without some form of rent book or receipt. Later I found that out no-one knew she rented an apartment; no wonder she wasn't prepared to have anything in writing. I still insisted on some form of receipt and eventually got one, although it never stated what the money was for.

I always refused to have anything to do with dishonesty. Had there been a showdown, I would have had no proof that I had paid any rent at all, and I'd already had the experience of people turning very nasty when it suited them.

The second problem came when I was never left alone. In all fairness to the owners, I suppose they thought, as so many people do, that everyone who is on their own is automatically lonely. This, thank God, has never been the case with me, but they couldn't accept it. As I was not coping so well at the office, my time off in the evenings and at weekends was vital to me for peace and quiet. But directly I returned home, I was either rung for or, if I didn't appear was yelled for from outside the house. The family had plenty of rows and were constantly shouting at each other, so no way could I get away from it. At weekends the son did some shooting from the grounds. I felt I'd jumped out of the frying-pan into the fire.

The third problem - which I had already experienced in other situations - was that someone was nosing about in my belongings. I had my suspicions, so set a very simple trap and kept an account of how often that person came in. It was rather too often for my liking.

Soon at the office, other signs began to show themselves which I found very alarming. I found I could no longer change from working the switchboard to typing without making awful errors which necessitated retyping the entire work. I had lost my train of thought and was unable to concentrate. All this frightened me, as my brain went completely blank, and I had to wait a second before I could reconnect. This had all happened in the past and it was quite clear it was going to happen again. After three years in this good job, the old symptoms were again very evident.

'Oh God, why does this always happen to me, just when I'd hoped to be settled at last!'

Within a year I'd moved again. This time the apartment was unfurnished so I bought the barest necessities. At least I was left alone and had a proper rent book.

As a relaxation, a friend and I started ice skating. I found it great fun especially after finding my balance. One day, as I was growing bolder and rather too fast for a beginner, I fell flat on my face continuing across the ice on my tummy. I thought nothing of that 'trip' until around 10 days later when I woke up one morning and could hardly breathe for the pain. Visiting a doctor I had some X-rays which revealed severe bruising. It was a long time before I could breathe happily without the sharp pain.

Of course there was a blaring radio all the time while we went round the ice rink. I have often wondered why noise has such a devastating effect on me; I can take so much, and then it is as though four walls in my head are caving in and I have to escape from the noise before the walls finally collapse on me. Any continual noise has the same effect. The louder it is, the sooner those inner walls start caving in. Perhaps this is why I've always loved silence and solitude. But it's frightening as in today's world as everything is perpetual noise. To find this silence that I seek and enjoy seems only now to be off the beaten track. Slowly, the bad signs built up more and more at the office, and my headaches grew worse. I knew there would have to be yet another change. In fact I came face to face with the truth, I could no longer take the pace and pressure of living in New York.

There was also another growing awareness that before long I would be given clear guidance concerning my future. Where or what I didn't know; but I sensed the doors were finally closing and I would soon be flying away again. In readiness, I found people who would buy my few possessions when the time came as I wanted to reduce everything down to my usual two suitcases. All was in mental readiness when the Lord clearly told me the doors were just about to close. There was absolutely no doubt about what I was told to do: I had to return to England.

When the time came, it was a terrible wrench. I knew it would be. But I realised my mental health was now at stake and which was the more important? Which was of more value, money or mind? I didn't stop to consider for one moment. So I entered another turn on the Turntable; another groove going to I knew not where. There was no other way, only His way and, although I hated the thought of returning to England, I knew I had to follow my Leader. My notice was given and my few remaining possessions sold to various friends.

On 15 July 1968, I flew back to England with my two suitcases. It was 'goodbye' to the four wonderful seasons, spring, summer, autumn and winter, that the State of New York had always provided. How I had loved each one.

Chapter 7

I was now faced with another waiting time. There was no doubt it had been right to return to England but there was plenty of doubt as to what I should do until I received further orders.

But how different this waiting time was compared with the last one; how I had grown in grace as well as in faith. What patience I now had in comparison and, above all, what peace. I not only recognised the inner voice much more clearly, but was sensing so much more in advance. Nothing was ever revealed to me clearly but a great awareness of things to come now came with assurance. Never have I been given any time factor in these matters, I just have to wait until I know the time is right. I no longer wanted to reason everything out with common sense, I was accepting things without so many questions such as 'why,' and 'I don't understand.' So often I've hated what I've known I had to do and have to admit I've done more than my share of grumbling.

Settling down was definitely out. I knew I was going to be kept on the move, more or less, for a considerable time yet. I just hoped God's plans would take me abroad again.

Again, I made my base at my mother's flat. Poor Mummy, she never understood the amazing way of life I led, and I couldn't explain it either. How could I say what I was planning to do next when I was awaiting instructions from above? Only those who have received such guidance will know what I'm talking about. I'd given up planning years ago. Now I waited for the next turn on the Turntable.

When doubt crept in, I remembered the past. Hadn't I experienced that wonderful thrill of God's protection and provision? Had there ever been a time after a waiting period that He had not proved my walk was in accordance with His will? Even the uneventful wait was all in order. So I had to wait, and wait I would. I was sure that in this seemingly very odd way of life, without putting down any roots, the Lord had a specific way mapped out for me and me alone. pre-prepared in eternity.

The more I have the Lord in my life, the more I want Him the Lord of my life. It matters not whether I'm thought of as odd, eccentric, or anything else in the sight of men. In my constant search for this all-wonderful Lord I am ready to count things as nothing if I can delve into the depths which are to be found in Him. I know the cost is great. I know I kick and scream. But deep down in my heart I know I want no other way. The joy of finding His hidden treasures far outweigh (in the long run) what I have had to let go of and relinquish. So I prepared myself to wait in the groove, until the next turn was shown me on the Turntable. I had to wait seven months.

It took me some time to re-adjust to the sudden change of pace and living; only after my return did I realise just how fast and furious my life had become; but how unhappy I was back in England. The climate was so dull and dismal in comparison. How I missed the sun, and the outgoing way of life. Oh dear! This is the very area where I kick against God's will the most; my constant longing to live where my heart says 'you're home'. It has happened twice only in the whole of my life; Austria and, later, New Zealand. So much of my life has been like a grizzly child who knows the way he's being led is the right way but is reluctant to follow, so he drags on his Father's hand a step or two behind. How heavy the going is, both for Father and child. Don't we all experience it? Even as I write this book, I'm secretly longing for the Lord to open the door again so that once more I can go abroad. What a difference it makes when a happy child skips and bounces along at your side with joy, never questioning the leadership, or the decision. What patience our heavenly Father has with us all.

Soon after my return to England, I gave my name to an overseas agency for a job abroad. As nothing was forthcoming I thought I'd better look for a local job. Having far too much energy to sit around, and receiving no definite guidance, I searched the local job centre. I also needed some money again.

The only type of job I could take was domestic work; as my future was so uncertain I thought it wouldn't be fair to apply for permanent work. I found two jobs that were suitable; one, a part-time evening job in a posh school, the other in a children's home. I think both places were desperate for another pair of hands as there was no interview as such, just a 'when can you start?' I don't think they minded what sort of body owned the hands; they were desperate for almost any type of help. I don't mind housework but, if you sit down to work it out, the everlasting cleaning of other peoples' dirt can become boring, tiring, and depressing. Certainly it's very necessary work in life but never would I have chosen it as a career. I told people who questioned me as to why I did it, that it was always easy to pick up that kind of work. That was true enough but little did they know I kicked against it so often in my heart. One day in my daily reading, it was pointed out that the Lord was spending a lot of His time cleaning me! It certainly curtailed my constant complaining; for a time.

The evening job at the school was as follows: Four or five of us hovered around open canteen hatches like birds of prey, waiting to receive empty dishes from the girls' dining room where they were having their supper. The full dishes had already been passed through and set on the tables. Now we waited for the refills. A couple of men stood at enormous deep sinks, full of hot suds ready to begin the mammoth task of washing up.

It was a very posh school; for gentry, moneyed people, would-be ladies? But, being on the serving end as usual and in spite of our snowy white overalls, things hadn't really changed much since I began that kind of work all those years ago. We were the servants and there was the 'you are serving us' sort of attitude. Items were shoved through the hatches at us with utterances like 'butter,' or 'more potatoes,' or 'I don't like that meat; ask chef if I can have an egg.' I had expected a 'please' or a 'thank you,' those dear little words my mother had taught us would-be ladies at home.

'Do your parents know you speak like this, or have you acquired these manners since you've been here?' I asked of one girl as an empty butter plate came hurtling through the hatch at me with the order, 'more butter!' I waited for a meek little 'please' which was faintly heard above the din of the dining-room, and the clatter of cutlery in the kitchen, before I let go of the plate, now amply refilled with butter. A lily-white hand took it gently from me. The next time she encountered me through the hatch there was a marked difference in the young lady's approach.

After the girls had left the dining-room, my job was to collect and wash up the cups. I whisked them off the tables onto a large trolley then speedily wheeled the trolley to another room where the most marvellous washing machine stood at my disposal. The machine was circular; the cups were laid inside in large round baskets which revolved at high speed after the hood had been lowered and the start button pressed. Inside, all around the baskets, jets of water were released, and with a loud whooshing sound they shot up under great pressure and heat. At the end of the cycle, if I lifted the hood directly the whooshing had stopped, a great cloud of hot steam rushed heavenward and I was in time to see the baskets still whizzing around before they came to a standstill. The cups were boiling hot at this point and hardly touchable. Naturally, I was shown the workings of this remarkable machine, with the warning: 'Always make sure the hood is pulled down before you press the start button!' Honestly, just as though I'd do anything so stupid.

Once clean - and sterilised - the cups were returned to the trolley and I wheeled them back to the dining-room where they were placed upside down on saucers ready for the girls' breakfast. I did so enjoy working that machine. Week by week my speed increased. I flew back and forth with great efficiency, finishing ever earlier to the amazement of the others. 'Nobody's ever done it so fast,' I was told. One evening, however, I stood by my old pal, the cup machine, with confidence and pride. But the Lord had a little plan up His sleeve that I didn't know anything about. I still don't know how it happened but, somehow, my inner mechanism went wrong. The hand that lowered the hood became confused with the hand that pressed the start button. Each was confused as to who should enter the race first. The start button won. With an almighty whoosh, the jets of hot water hit the ceiling, drenching me in their descent. I watched the cups spinning round on a roundabout in a dry and thirsty land. By the time I'd mentally switched on, I managed to switch off the machine. Alas, it was already too late. I was soaked. My pride melted in the heavenly hot water that had come down, my hair hung limp and lifeless, and my overalls clung close to my body, revealing many hidden curves! But there was no time to stop; the work had to be finished. Starting up the machine (this time with the hood down) I wiped the walls and floor as best I could, but ignoring the dripping ceiling. When my work was finished I joined the others in saturated silence. I thought the roof would come down with their laughter. No more did I try to be the quickest and smartest cup-washer-upper the school had on record, especially after the Lord had seen fit to douse His daughter down.

The other job, at the nursery school, was a complete antithesis. My work involved washing, ironing, folding and putting away the children's clothes. Each morning, I took the dry clothes from the lines in the drying room where I had hung them the previous day. I ironed what needed ironing, and then put the items (eventually) in the right piles on the shelves above the children's names. Then I collected all the dirty clothes from the day before, sorted them out according to colour etc, and started to wash them in the machines. When they were clean and spun, they were hung in the drying room. Every day presented the same routine. Sometimes I helped wash the children's hair.

The clothes were old, darned and faded but always clean. Woollens were mostly matted, sheets discoloured from constant wetting. They were poor children, some unwanted or abandoned; all colours, sizes and ages. But they were loved by the staff, well fed and cared for, and they seemed extremely happy. I couldn't help thinking that for some of them it would perhaps be the only decent home they would ever know. Some years later I went to revisit the home but found it had been pulled down to make way for road improvements. I wondered where all the children had gone.

One day, a phone call from the international agency informed me there was a job available with a family in Germany; was I interested? Interested! In a flash I knew this was the next move to take, so gave in my notice at both the rich and the poor houses. The staff were sorry I was leaving, but I had previously told them I had applied for an overseas post. Now another challenge stood before me, another launching out into the deep to let down my nets. Oh blessings upon blessings, there was no way of seeing what was on the Turntable for my immediate future. To me, it was just another adventure in the Lord.

In February 1969, I flew to Germany to my job. I went as a kind of au pair, a kind of old one at that. All had been arranged by the agency regarding pick-up at the airport. On my arrival I sat by my two suitcases, and waited for someone to come. My head was pounding with the old pain from tension and nerves.

Changing from one place to another, and from one job to another, can be very nerve-wracking. One walks totally into the unknown with almost all sense of security left behind. Changing countries, however, one enters another culture, another set of rules, another currency, and another climate, and this time, another language.

At first it can be disturbing. Even different food and drink can bring new problems. Also, when living in other peoples' homes, you have to adjust to their way of life. Homes may be lovely and the people very kind, but sometimes I found it impossible to adjust.

As I sat waiting to be picked up, I felt uneasy, but not unduly so. There were a lot of people milling around but one woman caught my eye. I knew instinctively she was Frau Jung. My heart sank into my boots. My head pounded in a new agony. My adrenalin did whatever it does when confronted with fright. I saw in a flash what I was ultimately to face during the next seven months or so of my stay. The expression on her face was terrifying. She passed by, and I felt momentarily relieved. You could have been wrong, I thought; relax! A long time passed and I was among only a few people left at the airport when a young man came to collect me. He spoke some English which was a help.

On arrival at the wealthy palatial house, I was introduced to Frau Jung. We shook hands. I had been right! I tried to make my home under this terrifying woman who ruled her family with an absolute frightening authority. It wasn't long before she thought I would also be included under her rule but, I hasten to add, she never succeeded. Why? Perfect love casts out fear. I had more than tasted the Lord's perfect love, and the amount I had was already eradicating fear of certain people.

Frau Jung was very patient with me as I helped her around the house, seeing she had no English and I very little German, in spite of all my studying. What I had learned was not adequate for every day conversation and getting about. I could neither ask questions properly, nor understand all she tried to tell me. Even our sign language didn't always suffice. I was treated by some of the older children as less than dirt. I felt as though I was deaf and dumb, experiencing the appalling frustration of not being able to express myself; the awfulness of not being understood, and the equal awfulness of not being able to understand. Never so far, had I felt so utterly cut off from everybody and everything. In time, as I was able to accept it, this frustration lessened. Did it really matter if no one could understand me? I began to laugh at all the mistakes I made.

It was a worldly home without love. All they had was money, and what money could buy. There was evidence of this throughout the entire house. A more loveless place I doubt existed anywhere. No one had time for anyone else but him or herself. Each would succeed, even if they trod on their neighbour and crushed them in the process. Just too bad, He was in my way! Above all this, there was a dominating woman, determined to have her success in all her children. I must have appeared a poor simple fool in comparison.

There was a piano which I asked if I could play occasionally. Of course I could. Having no music, and not being able to play by ear, I borrowed some simple pieces the children had. The books lay on top of the piano; there was also a hymn book. One day, I asked the young son if it was all right to play his music. He was studying the violin and practised elsewhere in the house so no doubt could hear me playing at times. 'I'm not a lending library!' came the curt reply. So I opened a hymn book and played every hymn I knew from the book. Day after day, I practised the hymns until finally the mother was singing them. So the hymn book had been freely given, not lent. Wasn't that lovely; worthless to the son, perhaps, but of great value to the One I was singing about.

The rows over politics were red hot. Never have I heard such shouting and yelling when the entire family came together at weekends. It always happened over meals. I dreaded those weekends and took more tablets for the headaches they brought on.

No one had time to explain things to me. 'Ask at meal times,' I was told. But how do you ask when you can't speak the language? However, someone understood; hadn't He known all this in advance? So I turned to Him, taking more and more time to be with Him. If I hadn't had the assurance that the Lord wanted me in that household, I would have left. But one day, early in my desperation, He said to me: 'I want your example here.' Later on, I realised He had made an escape for me. It was in my total lack of understanding what was said. It was impossible for me to become involved. So I was able to hold my peace in that Godless place. Haven't I already said, thank God it's only one groove at a time? But some of the grooves are very deep, and the Turntable turns at the slowest possible speed imaginable. In fact sometimes it appears to have stopped. There have been times when I thought things would never change.

One episode I remember above all the others. One of the daughters wanted me to go with her to the opera one evening. I don't like opera, so said I wouldn't go as I wanted to wash my hair. There was uproar as she wouldn't go alone. I thought nothing more about it. I finished clearing the table and washing up, then started to go upstairs to my room. Frau Jung met me half way up the stairs, barring the way. She demanded an explanation as to why I had refused to go with her daughter to the opera. So terrible was her expression, I expected flames to leap from her mouth. She was a very tall woman and towered above me at the best of times; a few stairs above me made her look like a giant. Looking her calmly in the face I said, 'Excuse me, I wish to go upstairs and wash my hair.' She meekly stepped aside without another word and let me pass by. As time went on, I learned a lot of German, but never let anyone know just how much I really understood. I preferred to live in my inner silent world.

As I had little money (I was paid a small sum), the best I could do for outings was to take a tram and look around the city of Cologne. On my first trip I was told what number tram to catch and where to get off. Except for the number, the name of the stop was mumble jumble. No one bothered to write it down for me so I thought, 'you're on your own girl, quit asking and go find your own way around,' and find out I did.

I managed to be in the right place when the right numbered Strassenbahn arrived, so got in. That to me was a great accomplishment, as everything seemed back to front, driving on the right side of the road again. What splendid trams they are, divided into two sections with a most wonderful circular plate inside connecting the sections, enabling it to swing round corners. It was such fun standing on that metal plate as it revolved.

After a most pleasant sightseeing trip, I found myself back where I'd started, and without paying. Not being told anything, I didn't know what to do. What I should have done of course, was to get into the front part, and drop my money in an amazing contraption which looked like a lantern, and ticked like a wheezy clock. Then I could choose to sit where I liked. No one had explained these things to me so, in all ignorance, I'd had a free ride. Another strange and remarkable thing I was soon to learn was the number of people who shouted at me. Why is it that, if someone doesn't understand what you say, they are automatically classified as deaf? I was to spend a lot of my early weeks in Germany in that social category.

Soon I was growing more adventurous, and had discovered that one could buy some tickets in advance which saved a bit of money. One day, I stepped onto a tram with great confidence, holding my ticket in my hand for the driver to see; I then proceeded to find a seat. In a matter of seconds, a multitude without number started shouting one word at me – 'Knipsen, knipsen!' I didn't need to rehearse my blank look as I thought by now it had more or less become permanent. I stood aghast, mouth wide, until I found the words, 'I'm English, I don't understand.' Immediately the shouting stopped. My audience turned from shouting to smiling in the twinkling of an eye. A kindly gentleman stepped forward and in impeccable English told me what to do. There was, it seemed, another contraption by the driver, that went 'ting ting' when the ticket was pressed into it; it re-emerged with a hole in it (I had learnt the hard way that knipsen meant punch, perforate). I felt most embarrassed that I couldn't speak the language; shame on us who don't ever try.

Another time I got into serious trouble as I'd changed trams on the same ticket. Not being able to read the minute instructions on the back in German, I didn't know what to do. An inspector got on and tried to explain what I had done wrong. I couldn't understand a word he said but he went on shouting at me. Finally, I paid the sum of 10 Deutschmark penalty but still without a clue as to where I'd gone wrong. A kind lady explained and was furious with the inspector for treating me so badly. I just accepted it as my lot in struggling to find my way around without the language.

Park seats also proved most interesting. A lot of people rested and chatted with each other on park seats. They drew me into conversation, and helped me a lot with many questions for which I needed answers. I always carried note paper and a pencil with me to jot things down. It's the only way I can remember. With all these things, plus my own private study, I began to make great headway with the language. I found walking around the stores and shops, listening to other people buying and selling, a unique way of learning.

Two incidents I noted in my diary.

On my return home one day I met a road sweeper with his barrow, not far from where I got off the tram. We fell into conversation. Well, I wanted to learn German didn't I? It didn't take me long to find out what he was trying to say but I pretended not to understand in spite of all his gesticulations. I put on my puzzled and blank look, knowing full well he wanted to make a date with me. Suddenly his face lit up. Pushing his coat sleeve up, a very large watch was revealed. I watched the hands whizzing around and the hours fly by. Heavens, it was now 7 o'clock! With one finger he pointed first to the hour, then to me, and then to himself, then finally, to the spot where we were standing. 'Ah ja,' I exclaimed, allowing myself a smile of comprehension, not consent! He looked so pleased. I wended my way back grinning to myself. Poor chap, I thought, how easily one can be misinterpreted in a foreign language. From then on, I always scanned the road carefully to see if there were any road sweepers loitering about with their barrows, or just loitering, before I bolted down the road to catch the tram.

The other incident concerned toilets; one of the first things I always find out in new cities is where they are located. I have to say that both in Germany and Austria toilets are the most delightful places; spotlessly clean, always with an attendant to polish the seat for you. They were not expensive, well worth a visit. One day, being in need, I walked into a toilet and, finding no attendant, I pulled open a door that was already ajar and went in. There was a funny kind of lock and when I went to shut the door, it didn't close properly; in fact there was a considerable gap for anyone to see the inmate. Quite undaunted I did what had to be done, then, to my horror found I couldn't get out; I was a prisoner, half in, half out. These were my early days in the country, and what does one do in an emergency when one hasn't the right words for the right occasion, especially in a new language? I hadn't even learned the German word for 'help' which I now seemed so desperately to need. So, pitching my voice above the sound of traffic and flushing loos, I let forth in fortissimo, 'I'm an English woman!' Well honestly, what would you have shouted in such a situation? A surly looking attendant appeared, peering at me through the gap and with the clank of heavy keys, released me from my half-in, half-out prison. An open hand awaited the unpaid fee.

I was meant to attend university in the mornings but, by the time I'd put the breakfast things in the dishwasher and caught the bus, I always arrived late. Then I could never find my way around and was so embarrassed having to walk in front of the large class when I did eventually find the room. There was always a great roar of laughter at my arrival. I never found out why. I never learnt anything and when we had dictation about the kind of fish the fishmonger was selling … well, that was my last day of attending university at Cologne. What a ridiculous subject to teach students who were desperately trying to make their way about in a foreign country. What good would it have done me had I shouted out, cod, haddock, hake, from my imprisonment in the German loo? I wonder if all foreign students are taught in this manner.

I had been in the family about six months when both parents went away for a month's holiday. Except for the daily cleaning woman, I was left alone to cope. All hell was let loose. The children (adults really) with their new found freedom did just what they pleased, and I couldn't blame them. But life became a worse misery. I was ordered about, shouted at, spoken to as if I was their servant (which, no doubt, I was), no one came to meals on time and never told me if they would be out, or wanted to eat at different times. If things weren't ready they complained, and I could reckon there would always be something wrong. I received little or no help. I remember one day, I sat down to the midday meal and started on my own as no one came on time. When the eldest member did arrived anyone would have thought I'd committed the horrendous crime ever. I lacked all manners, was rude, and hadn't a clue how to behave. What he hadn't seen, however, was his own wounded pride, that he had not succeeded in keeping me waiting. But my head was splitting and my heart breaking from the deepest inner misery. I tried to be gentle, loving and kind, bearing no animosity, but just finished up at night crying my heart out to the Lord. Very slowly I recognised the inner pressure; that this would soon be over and a change would take place.

I had given my word I would stay until the parents returned; anyway, I had nowhere to go. On the day of the parents' return, we had eaten the evening meal, and I had gone to my room after washing. Within a few seconds, I could hear voices yelling at each other three floors down. I knew the parents had returned. The children who were older in years but very childish in behaviour, having tasted freedom, refused to be chained again. I stayed upstairs, not even going down for a drink. I knew I just couldn't face any more. I had reached rock bottom again.

I was now faced with a ghastly decision. As the inner pressure increased, telling me I must leave, my 'sense of duty,' and 'my given word,' said I couldn't. I was severely tested. Whose word was I going to obey; mine or His? 'Oh God,' I cried, 'how can You ask me to go against my word, my promise? You said You wanted my example here. What sort of an example is it if I go against my promise to stay until the said date?' But the pressure to leave only increased, and became heavier and heavier, until I knew without a shadow of doubt I dared not disobey Him any longer.

A friend, with whom I had previously confided, said I could always go to her if the worst came to the worst. I phoned her to say I would be arriving the next day. I got up at 4'oclock the next morning, feeling like a convict escaping from a prison. Silently I moved about packing my suitcases. Stripping the bed, I left the linen folded in a neat pile at the bottom. I had hardly slept with the thought of what I was about to do. My head was fuzzy, and my eyes on stalks from crying. I was hardly aware of what I was doing. Well, I thought, this certainly is His and not my will being done. I would never have had the courage to do it without Him.

Going down to breakfast as usual, no one seemed to notice my flushed face and red eyes. After clearing the table and washing up, I went back to my room. Always having the morning free until midday, no one expected to know, or bothered, as to my whereabouts. Knowing the movements of everybody every day, I left my room in a clean and orderly manner, crept downstairs with my suitcases and out of the front door. Having phoned for a taxi, I sat on a suitcase outside on the pavement in a state of terrible nerves and guilt lest I should be discovered. It mattered not whether I lived or died at that moment. As the taxi drew up, I gave the driver the written address of my friend's house and almost fell inside with relief.

My heart was bursting with the agony of going against 'my' word. I had yet to learn that when the Lord speaks His commands to us personally, nothing and no one must stand against them. He is not concerned with our loyalty to our ideals, promises, notions and creeds, but the rightness of relationship and loyalty to Him, not what we think about Him. 'If you love Me, keep my commandments!' Why then, did I have this terrible sense of guilt? Was it perhaps that I would rather have hung on to my word because it was easier than what He had asked me to do? Had I forgotten that His thoughts are not our thoughts, and His ways are not our ways? Now I know that delay in doing his will is denial of Him. We believe in ourselves first, and have put Him second. Total obedience is very costly at times. The cost is more than we want to give, let alone do. He was teaching me that I had no rights to myself if I wanted to follow Him. He was claiming all. Was I prepared to give all?

My friend was out when I arrived at her house; I couldn't help it, I sat on her front door step and wept in desolation. What was I doing? Was I really under guidance, or was I just one of those people who imagine all this, simply because I couldn't see things through to the end? Great doubt began to take over. How I longed to be settled in a nice place like most people were, with a good job and income. That night came the consolation and assurance I needed from a book I unpacked from my suitcase (book title and author forgotten).

> 'Let there be no hurry. You live in eternity, not in, time. It is in the unseen that your future is being planned. This is the way of uncertain future, and faltering steps. It is MY way. Put all fear of the future aside. Know you will be led, know you will be shown. Have I not promised?'

How hard it is to trust in situations like this? We're out in the deep again, with no firm ground beneath us. The tempest rages; there is no proof or sign that we will reach the shore even when the storm abates. All we can see is blackness and hopelessness. There is no shape or form in this darkness. But once again I was to prove just how safe I was in His hands. He was manipulating me into the right place for the right time on the Turntable. The next groove had to be stepped into very quickly. Had I not been there, ready, waiting for the swiftness with which it would take place. Had I not obeyed the Lord's command and left the previous family when I did, someone on His 'waiting list' would have missed a great blessing. I would not have been there. The contact would never have been made, and future guidance perhaps lost for ever. And to think all this would have been missed because I thought my word was more important than His.

More and more, I was learning a reliance on the Lord when I couldn't see. Soon, I was going to move about with fewer headaches and nerves, simply because I was finally beginning to mistrust myself in my own decisions. I was now growing afraid to step out in my own wisdom. I was learning to understand that we cannot see as the Lord sees. We cannot see the consequences of our own actions however well planned. We think we can, but how many times have we met disappointment from our own actions. 'If only I'd known then what I know now,' we say. Could I now not begin to feel 'safe' when the tempest raged? Yes, that's exactly what was beginning to happen. He placed me in the depths to test me. What would be my reaction? To whom would I turn? Was He or was He not the 'pivot' holding my record on the Turntable? At last, I was beginning to grasp what He was trying to teach me. Slowly, this 'grasp' began to take hold.

Chapter 8

My first job was to tell the agency what I had done; not a pleasant task. I took a tram to somewhere near the agency's offices, got off and became completely lost. I had to ask someone the way. Three men were walking towards me so I approached one of them and showed him a slip of paper with the agency's details and address. He beamed from ear to ear. 'I know the lady well, I'll escort you there myself', he said. Do I need mention he spoke perfect English? I was duly taken to the lady herself at the agency where, with a click of his heels, a hand shake and a slight bow, he took his leave.

The lady accepted what I'd told her. 'Is there another job in the area?' I asked. Nothing whatsoever I was told. I would have to go to another city. But deep inside me I knew I had heard the word 'wait.' So I turned down all the other excellent jobs elsewhere that were offered me. I felt by now that the agency lady had lost all interest. 'I'll wait one week,' I said. 'Here's my telephone number where I am staying, just in case a job comes up in this area.' She reiterated that there was nothing, and implied that the idea of waiting was rather stupid, especially as there were so many good jobs elsewhere. But so clear had the word 'wait' come into my heart, I was prepared to do just that and see what the week would bring.

In fact I only had to wait two days. On the second day, I returned to my friend's house in the evening to find a telephone number waiting for me to ring. It was the agency. 'They have been trying to reach you all day,' my friend said. Ah-ha, I thought, here we go. I dialled the number. Apparently, a girl from another country had been booked to care for a family but at the last moment she was not allowed to travel. The family that had contracted her was desperate. Was there anybody in the vicinity who could help them? Well of course there was. There was I, ready and waiting to fill the gap. Before I even phoned the lady, I had received my inner orders. 'You are to take this job.' And where do you think this lady and her family lived? If you don't believe it you must. It's just a few streets away. Later I walked to her house after telling her over the phone I would gladly come. The next day - in the glorious autumn of 1969 - I moved in. Lovelier people I couldn't have found anywhere. It was my joy to serve them.

For whatever reason, I feel I must include in detail what happened during my stay with this family. I cannot explain, understand nor give any reason why the following took place, so I'm simply rewriting it as I wrote it in my diary. It was to be one of the richest and most wonderful periods of my life.

Ever since being with this new family, Frau Amsel laid heavily on my heart, so much so that at times I haven't been able to sleep. I pray deeply I love this lady as I've never loved a lady before. There is nothing sexual about this love, just an overwhelming 'oneness' I have for her. I know this is mutual, although I've never spoken to her about it. I cannot describe the tremendous 'inflowing' I've received without ceasing for five weeks now. It's so beautiful; it's like an anointing of absolute beauty, peace and tranquillity. I am bursting with its fullness.

> *From my diary - Friday 7 November 1969*
> 'I went to my room, having finished my work. My room is downstairs in the basement, but has a door leading outside. The ground has been cut away in front of my window so there is plenty of light and air. (Later, I planted pansies there and enjoyed the heavenly scent that wafted from them into my room.) I also have a wash basin and toilet off the room.
>
> 'As I pottered around I was suddenly given a vision, a picture, call it what you will on my inner screen. I saw before me a very, very steep climb, up a mountain side. Right over the edge, clinging to what appeared to be a rope, was a figure which I knew represented Frau A. I knew the climb would be long, slow and a dreary one, but the ascent was sure. There was no doubt about it. We were together and we were going up.

'Frau Amsel was in a very poor health at the time of my arrival. The signs of many things that took place made me form my own opinion as to the nature of her illness but not being in the medical profession I kept my opinion to myself. To this day, I never knew what was really wrong with her.'

Tuesday 18 November
'Today, I see the figure on this steep slope is moving. No longer is it still, but is struggling on the rope to which it is clinging. What a wonderful change is taking place in Frau A. I watch a new strength and faith. Instead of fear, joy is beginning to show its face. The effect on the whole family is marvellous to see. '

Friday 21 November
'After three days watching this figure struggling, today the entire position has changed. The figure is quite still, with arms above its head. It is no longer over the edge, but is gently coming toward the firm ground of the mountain side. Whatever the figure has hold of is held firmly in its hands. It is looking downwards towards the place where its feet will land.'

Saturday 22 November
'There is more movement in the figure today. It is looking up and down, and I note some anxiety in its face. The feet are just above the ground. Every day, I watch the wonderful change in Frau A as we work and talk together during the day. My joy is so great, I feel I could burst!'

Sunday 23 November
'Last night, I saw the figure touch the ground for a second then come off again. Tonight, both feet are placed on the ground. Now I see her face clearly. She is looking around but I see no fear in her expression. Although the rope is still in her hands, it is not taut, and her arms are no longer held above her head. Her face is

towards me now, and very clear.'

Thursday 27 November
'The figure is beginning to move. She has turned away from me, so I can no longer see her face.'

Sunday 30 November
'I see considerable movement in the figure again. Although her back is towards me, the way seems much flatter. For the first time I notice colour; green and brown. Also God's word came to me. 'She must climb alone.' What marvellous evidence there is to see in Frau Amsel. Everything I see in the vision is verified in her life. I cannot express the compassion and love I am experiencing.'

Monday 1 December
'I am standing alone. The figure has walked so far ahead, she is in the distance. Strange! It has not become smaller, in fact if anything it is bigger than before. She is walking on and on with her back towards me so I can't see her face. The way appears flat and straight.'

Tuesday 2 December
'I don't understand. The figure has grown out of all proportion. It is enormous and now seems to be right in front of me. I feel squashed, suffocated, engulfed by it. It's rather frightening.'

Sunday 14 December
'There has been no change in the vision since the last entry. The figure remains standing with me - very large indeed.'

I spent my first Christmas in Germany with this family. It was a lovely time. We all opened presents on Christmas Eve. I received a lovely cuckoo clock, a thing I'd always wanted. (Actually, the cuckoo all but drove me mad; I had to lock him in his house so he couldn't cuckoo every hour all night long. I heard the whirring behind his closed door but the poor chap could not make an appearance).

My sister from London (Audrey) came for a four-day holiday. We visited Bad Godesberg and the environs. What a lovely place it was. I remember she slept in my bed, and Frau Amsel gave me a camp bed. It was so hard to lie on and would have kept tipping up if I hadn't sat squarely in the centre. I was please to get back to my own soft bed when my sister left.

I also met a girl who had been in my form at school. She and her husband lived close by and I attended the little English-speaking church where her husband was padre. Once a week I was allowed to practice on the small organ there. It was quicker to find out what it couldn't do, but with all the stops out, perhaps six at the most, it was a great outlet and relaxation for me to crash around on the one manual with any music I could find. I spent a half-day a week playing that organ then enjoying a jam doughnut with coffee in a nearby restaurant. It all brought great joy to me. My day off took me further a field.

Frau Amsel spoke many languages. I owe the German that I spoke to her kind and careful training. Everything was explained to me so graciously. We went shopping and for walks together with the children. If I went shopping alone, she insisted the list was written in German. I must admit that this was the best and fastest way to learn a language. What a contrast to the first family.

> *Monday 19 January 1970*
>
> 'The figure is moving again. I am also aware and believe I'm coming to the end of something; another change? It's not yet clear, only awareness. This 'something' seems to be appearing as a big blanket of grey-white mist in the distance. It seems ominous. Today it's coming towards me but still is not clear. I'm afraid of it. I feel it will bring sadness. I doubt my very own thoughts at this moment, yet deep down, I think I know what is going to happen. I have no fear of not being able to cope, only the struggle of going through it.'

Thursday 29 January

'God spoke to me through His word. 'I clear the path. Have no fear; you must know that all is well. I will never let anyone do to you, other than my will for you. I can see the future. I know better than you what you need. Trust Me absolutely. You are being let in a very definite way and others, who do not serve your purpose, are being moved out of your path by Me. Never fear whatever may happen. All is for the best for you.' What a comfort and assurance this was. It was a heavy path I trod. I had the care of three children, all the household duties, plus the load that had been spiritually laid upon me. Later, I noticed the blanket of cloud had gone.'

Tuesday 10 February

'The path appears to be completely blocked today by a very large object. I can't say what it is but it is right in front of me. It's very big and high, and I can't see past it; otherwise it has no shape.'

Thursday 12 February

'The object has become a building. What? Where? I don't know. I see the figure standing on a very high spot absorbing the view below her.'

Friday 6 March

'The figure is still in the same place.'

The next day, I was told Frau Amsel had gone into hospital. She phoned in the evening sounding very upset.

We had had many wonderful discussions together over many things and I had told her a little about my life. Many times, she would go downstairs and rest in my room where it was quiet. She always had to have so much quiet each day. My Bible and daily readings were left on the dressing table and I often wondered if she ever opened the book and read it. I felt now I had to tell her about myself and what the Lord had done for me.

Some days after she had gone into hospital (I never knew why), I'd finished my work and went downstairs to my room. As I got into bed, I saw the face of a woman close by me. The face was haggard, pale and very thin. It was so awful I put my hands over my eyes in the hope of shutting out the picture but of course it didn't work as it was really on my inner screen. I tried not to think about it and eventually fell asleep. Posting my letter I'd now written, I continued with my daily duties with the children, cooking and everything during Frau Amsel's absence.

A week later, I was in the kitchen with the fridge door open when I heard her voice in the hall. I had been told she was coming home. It was a very high fridge, so I did not see her as she came into the kitchen. I turned around and she hugged me saying how good it was to see me again. It was not until she loosened her grasp that I was able to see her face. I had the shock of my life. It was the face I'd seen that night in my room. I was horrified at the change. She looked ghastly, so thin, and oh, so white. But there was a light in her eyes that told me something else. 'I've waited six years for someone to tell me what you told me in your letter,' she said. We hugged each other again.

'Why didn't you ask me?' I questioned.

'I couldn't,' she replied, 'why didn't you tell me?' she said.

'I wanted to be sure you really wanted to know about the Lord,' I replied.

I lent her my daily readings. Never in my life had I met anyone so hungry for the word of God. She just couldn't get enough, sitting with me to question this and that as she read through. At around 9.30 one evening, a tremendous load was removed from me.

Another place I used to go in my time off was along the Rhine. It fascinated me to watch the cargo being pushed along the river. According to my slides, it was in 1969 that the river rose and flooded the area. I watched it become a lake and I think many low-lying houses had their basements flooded. When it eventually subsided, the debris remained in the huge trees. It was hard to believe it had risen to the height where the trees had streamers flying in their branches. What a powerful element water is and what irreparable damage it can do.

On 20 March, I flew to England for three weeks' holiday. It was while I was there, I realised how deeply involved I had become with Frau Amsel and her family. Actually, it frightened me as I knew the pain of leaving would be great. Yet inwardly, I felt I must try and withdraw a little but didn't know how to do it.

I returned to Germany on 19 April. It was a very dull day when we took off from Heathrow but soon we were flying above the clouds in glorious sunshine. There was a thin blanket of cloud with huge cumulus piling high in the sky, whose bases lay in the mist below. It gave the appearance of a huge lake with shadows of the clouds on it; quite a wonderful sight. Losing height, we bumped through the mist and cloud and it grew darker and darker. Suddenly we were in a heavy snow storm but the brilliant orange colour of the sun shone through the clouds and mist, flooding the wet roads beneath with its light.

It was so wonderful to be back in Germany. How I loved that country. My German had greatly improved and was becoming my first language. I seldom had to translate into English in my head, so this made me fluent. I found Frau Amsel much better but I knew there was only one road ahead of me, and that was downhill.

Monday 4 May 1970

'The vision is with me again! I see a great vast plain of emptiness.'

I was by now so involved with Frau Amsel and her sickness, whatever it was, I felt helpless to help her any more. She had again been in hospital and knew the end was in sight. But just how it would end I didn't know. Her mother had now come to live in the house.

Sunday 10 May

'The figure in this vast space has become so small I can hardly see it. In some strange way it has shrunk. I wonder if this means she's fading out of my life, or I'm fading out of hers. The thought makes me very sad.'

Monday 11 May

'Upon waking, I see the figure has completely disappeared. There is just a vast empty space with nothing to see.'

I got up that morning feeling so ill and sick at heart. Had she died in the night? Oh God, help me if she has. I set the breakfast table as usual for all of us. Frau Amsel did not arrive. I asked after her and was told she had gone away. Beyond this I was told nothing and again it was not my place to inquire. My heart could have burst with grief as I knew from the vision I would never see her again and no one had given me the opportunity to say 'goodbye or 'thank you.'

I never did see that dear lady again. I do not even know if she is still alive. Although my heart was breaking at the thought of leaving, I knew it was right. My work there was obviously finished.

An unfortunate incident brought about my departure more quickly than I anticipated. No one wanted to hear my side of the story. I knew Frau Amsel's mother did not like me. I think her daughter's nearness to me made her jealous, so she wanted me out of the house. Herr Amsel never interfered. I went out on my half day to play the little organ which did not bring consolation to me, eating my doughnut and drinking coffee in the restaurant, big solitary tears dropped onto my plate. I was broken hearted I had to leave Germany. I knew the doors had closed on that side of the Channel.

I had only one request before I finally left, and God granted me that request. I just wanted to write to Frau Amsel to say 'thank you' for all she had done for me. I knew no one would give me her address. 'Please Lord, give me the address somehow, so I can write my 'thank you' letter.' A few days later, Herr Amsel verbally gave his mother-in-law the telephone number where Frau Amsel was staying. Miraculously I remembered it. Next day, when I was alone, I searched the telephone directory until I found it, and an address. Then I wrote my 'thank you' letter and posted it. I told no one.

On 22 May 1970, the day of my departure, Frau Amsel's mother gave me a slip of paper with a reference on it 'in the name of my daughter.'

Standing on the platform waiting for the train, I read it, then tore it into a thousand pieces and threw it in a waste bin. 'In the name was about the only bit of truth in it! Herr Amsel just said he was very sorry it had come to this. Maybe he was powerless to do anything. I got on the train for England with a sad and very heavy heart.

Chapter 9

On my return to England, I put my name down with another agency offering to help people in need but for no longer than one month at a time. As always, I needed money but in the back of my mind I was hoping to go abroad again.

Having no car, I travelled by train to see my clients. Everything was paid for by the employer. You lived in their home as companion, dog's body, slave, or whatever was needed. Sometimes I had the use of their car for shopping and far, far worse, to drive them about. They were all back-seat drivers, all too ready to brake and change gear when they thought it necessary. The truth was that they hated other people using their cars and expected you to drive exactly as they did. On paper, these jobs sounded lovely; they were well paid, but in reality there were very many prblems.

As usual, you did the adjusting to their timetable, routine and pettiness. Everything ran like clockwork, to the hour, to the minute, to the second in almost every detail. You could be out somewhere, enjoying a ride, but couldn't continue as lunch was punctually at one o'clock. Any afternoon drive broke into the 'cup of tea at three!'

'Doesn't leave much time does it? Perhaps we'll wait until we have more time.' Have you noticed old people never have any time?

With the constant changing of kitchens, I could never remember where things were kept. Cooking was, of course, essential. Sadly, I loathe the job and I'm not very good at it simply because I have little interest in it. How wonderful it would be if we could eat one pill a day and feel fully satisfied. But alas, for most of the people I worked for, eating was one of their favourite pastimes, regardless of the consequences, and how many there were.

A lot of my time was spent waiting at chemists for potions, remedies, laxatives, etc. Each day, the medicines had to be administered; before meals, with meals, after meals, crushed or uncrushed, at night, with milk, without milk, as the case may be. They came as liquids, thick and thin, coloured or colourless. Tablets were all colours, some highly decorative in little plastic cases, all shapes and sizes, some reminded me of the hundreds-and-thousands Mummy used to put on the top of iced cup cakes. The bottles of medicine were usually grouped on a tray with glass and spoon at the ready.

On the cooking side, though, my stews and baked potatoes were a great success. I usually threw in everything I could find in the larder; nothing like a lot of onion for flavouring. Even a teaspoon of honey was sometimes included; delicious. But I was soon informed that 'certain things became too well lubricated.' So it was out with the onions, never out with the laxatives!

Another problem was that some of the beds I was left to sleep in left a lot to be desired. Certainly, they had magnificent head boards of walnut, mahogany and oak, and fancy posts at the bottom which loved to leave huge bruises on my thighs every time I just didn't quite make it past them, but the springs had sprung over the decades. Some creaked and nearly all sagged. It was nothing for me to wake up with backache. How do sailors fare in hammocks?

The times were many when I raided airing cupboards or other beds for extra pillows or blankets, anything that raised the valley to a plateau.

The biggest problem, however, was the constant raising of one's voice to be heard. The radio and television would be at full blast until my ears and head seemed to vibrate. I would sneak upstairs and put in some earplugs. Then my clients had to contend themselves with a companion who constantly cupped her hand behind her ear saying, 'sorry, I didn't quite catch what you said.'

Television was the bane of every household; night after night, whether you wanted it or not, you were compelled to sit and watch and listen to it. I found it purgatory. Just try and look interested when you are bored to tears. I could hardly say, 'excuse me, I think I'll spend the evening in my room.' I was their temporary companion, even if they had to raise their voices to reach me in my ear-plugged sanctuary. Anyway, I could hardly disappear; supper was at eight - sharp!

When I think of the hours of wasted time - I speak for myself - that I've had to spend looking and listening to a television night after night. Being a great reader, and not having the powers of concentration to shut out the extraneous noise, I relied on knitting and crochet to alleviate the nightly boredom. (It was years before I had a television set and then I'm so selective I wonder why I have one).

Most of the clients were very kind and most appreciative. Others were indifferent, while the remainder were absolutely terrible. However it was work, income and somewhere to live during the interim period while I grew more and more homesick to return to the Continent.

I did have one rather nightmarish experience in the house of an elderly man, but not with him personally. The house was very old and beautiful, with low beams and old oak doors that had wooden latches. To open the doors from the outside, one had to pull a piece of string which disappeared through a tiny hole and pulled up the latch on the other side. The house was in the country and stood in its own grounds with a mile-long driveway. The wind howled every day; the atmosphere terrified me, and the room I slept in filled me with unknown fears. It was very small with a very small window; I think it must have been a dressing-room or something at one time. It was so small there was hardly enough room to enter. At night, I made sure the door was bolted; this was strange as I seldom bolt myself in anywhere because of a strong claustrophobic feeling. In that room, I found sleep almost impossible. I twisted and turned, got up and looked out of the window, slept with my head at the other end of the bed. I tried everything to rid myself of this fear but it remained throughout my stay. I could not explain the fear and did not know how to deal with it.

While at this house, the old man was good enough to let me have some refresher driving lessons. It was ages since I'd last driven. In that time, traffic had greatly increased on English roads and, in addition, everything was on the other side of the road compared to the Continent. But as soon as I sat at the driving wheel with a large L on the roof above me, I soon remembered how to shift gears. I had three driving lessons in all but my reactions were still sluggish.

However, short, quiet driving trips went well at first; I took the old man shopping and to his hairdresser. Then one day he announced he wanted to go into Bristol. I had reason to worry, not least as the old man had a habit of shouting 'stop' just where he intended to get out, regardless of what was behind us. Yelling 'stop' might have been all right in the country, but not in the centre of a city.

The great day arrived, we were both stressed and I think neither of us really trusted the other. As soon as we got into the car, I realised the calibre of the back seat driver next to me. I was even shown where the ignition key went, and which way to turn the key. My driving, I was soon to discover, was either too fast or too slow, and most things didn't please his lordship. But off we went; backseat driver beside me making me ever more nervous. Being only five feet tall, I had to sit on cushions with the driving seat right forward so I could reach the pedals. That meant the steering wheel all but made grooves in the tops of my legs. Also, I prefer to see above the steering wheel rather than through it. Few people understand these problems experienced by the short in stature, and this man was no exception. The journey into Bristol went without a hitch but on the way back I ran into deep trouble. The problem involved a roundabout; instinctively to me, all the traffic was coming from the wrong direction as I had not yet fully readjusted to driving on the left. Confusion reigned in my head. Perhaps you are good at seeing exit signs with a third eye, while the other two eyes are glued to the road? Well, I'm not, neither was my passenger. We entered the roundabout race. It was while I was on the first lap that my orders came in a mighty bellow. 'Right, left, up, down, in, out.' What was he saying? I just can't remember. All I knew was that I couldn't change lanes because of the traffic and I happened to be in the wrong lane for the correct exit. We entered the roundabout for the second time; I tried in vain to see the right sign for the right exit and to be in the right lane at the right time. I not only had bellows from my irate passenger but hand signals as well pointing out the directions. All this would have been the answer had the old man not suffered from very bad arthritis which had so disfigured his fingers that they all pointed either in an outward or inward direction. So when he indicated the way out, it was impossible to gauge which way was 'this is the way, drive ye in it!' Yes, you've guessed it; we entered the roundabout for a third time. By now, I had a madman beside me bawling and bellowing like a chained lion, and a mad woman chauffeur about to explode because she was being bawled at. Having been treated as an imbecile from the start, not even capable of turning the ignition key in the right direction, what did he expect on a roundabout?

The detail is still unclear but at sometime I must have been released from the roundabout and I soon found a quiet lay-by where I let my passenger have it full blast! 'How dare you shout at me,' I said. 'If I shouted at you as you've shouted and bawled at me, you would call the agency and have me removed immediately. Well, it happens to work both ways with me. I respect you, and I expect respect from you, and what's more, you need never ask me to drive you anywhere again in spite of your kindness in giving me refresher driving lessons.' With that, I restarted the engine, and we drove back to the house in the most exquisite silence. I never sat in his car again.

In the New Year of 1971, I recognised that inner pressure again. What did God have in mind? What did He want to tell me? I listened very attentively as I didn't want to miss one word. The more we listen, the more acute becomes our hearing, or so I've found. Slowly Austria seemed to be forming in my mind. I had no specific word to confirm it, just a growing inner assurance that it was the country the Lord was laying on my heart. But where in Austria, how could I find a job, a place to live? What a mighty challenge this all seemed. I thought back to the wonderful guidance I received when I was led to the children's home in Valhalla, New York. Wasn't that after I'd left my job? After I'd burnt my boats behind me as they say? So, why couldn't He do that again for me? But was I prepared to launch out and let Him do it?

In faith, I now accepted the country of Austria as the place the Lord wanted me to go, but where in Austria. Would He please name the place as I hadn't a clue. Making an inquiry at a travel bureau I found I could enter the country on my British passport, then look for a job. It all seemed very frightening. Until now, I'd always had the security of a home to go to. Now, it appeared, I was expected to go to a country that was completely strange to me, without a job, or even knowing where I would lay my head. What a gigantic step in faith this would be on my part. Could I really trust the Lord? Did I really know Him well enough to do this? Was what He had already demonstrated to me regarding guidance and provision sufficient to motivate me in faith? Was I willing? Thinking of the holiday in 1959 when my eldest sister (Monica) and I stayed in Innsbruck, I thought perhaps that was the place I should go to. 'Shut the door if I'm wrong Lord, as I'm heading for Innsbruck.'

Suddenly, I remembered a little book we had bought for information on Austria before setting off on holiday. By now I was staying with my mother again in Bexhill and I searched everywhere for it there but without success. So sure was I by now that I would be going abroad, I'd finished with the agency.

Later I took a train to Eastbourne in search of the little book. I looked in many stores and book shops when, sure enough, there it was on a shelf with other holiday books. Opening it at random, one name stood out on most of the pages. I flipped through it and the same place seemed to be mentioned everywhere: Salzburg. The more I browsed through the book the more Salzburg appeared on almost every page. Now I felt sure the city had been pin-pointed for me but, as I went to a travel bureau to enquire about getting there, I asked for double proof as, for me, this was to be an unbelievable step into the depths of the unknown. 'Please Lord, give me a final confirmation that Salzburg is the city You want me to go to so there can be no doubt in my mind,' I asked.

Wandering around, I was a travel bureau further down the road and had barely opened the door when a huge poster almost jumped out at me from the opposite wall. Across the top of it, written in huge capitals was one word – SALZBURG. I felt as if someone had hit me from behind, and an inner voice said, 'why are you so slow to believe?' Enquiring the price of a one way air ticket, I left the bureau with a heart as light as a feather. I was setting off again to the country I'd fallen in love with all those years ago.

'I'm going to Salzburg,' I informed my mother on my return to her flat.

'I thought you said you were going to Innsbruck,' she answered.

'I did, but now I'm going to Salzburg.' Poor Mummy, I don't think she ever understood me although she lived to be nearly 91 years old. How could I have ever explain to her what had happened? It all sounded so crazy to the unbeliever and I hardly understood it myself. I was sad that I couldn't share things with her but on that I felt we were poles apart.

Later that same week, I bought a one-way air ticket to Salzburg for travel on 24 February 1971. At the time there was a postal strike; communications had come to a halt. The man at the travel bureau actually tested my faith to its limits although he never knew it. I just wish I could be treated like a grown-up, or that I could learn to keep my mouth shut. Just why I shared with him my intentions I don't know but when he heard I hadn't a job to go to, let alone somewhere to live, he insisted I took a return ticket. 'What will happen if you can't find somewhere to live, can't find a job, run out of money, can't contact anyone because of the postal strike?'

'But I've only been told to go to Salzburg, not come back,' I argued. Was I going to play safe with commonsense, or did I really trust the Lord? This was the greatest test so far in my walk on the Turntable. I decided to launch out into the deep and let down my nets in complete faith that it would be filled with overflowing bounty. The bounty was there all right, but I had to go with open, empty hands to receive it. I was prepared to be deemed a fool yet again for Christ's sake. And oh, was my foolishness rewarded? I think the man at the bureau believed he had a mule the other side of the counter but the mule anyway left his shop with a one-way ticket for Salzburg.

Do you realise there is a reckless abandon to God that is safer than all your reckoning; freedom to move in His will and ways without fear of the future? I was just beginning to enter that wonderful knowledge that God's foolishness is the wisest wisdom anyone could follow.

I arranged for a taxi to pick me up at 6.45 am on 24 February outside my mother's flat, there would be plenty of time to get to Heathrow for my flight at 11 am. Saying goodbye to Mummy, I carried my two suitcases down the stairs and stood outside the flat well before time. The taxi never turned up until later; it had waited at the wrong house further up the road. Already my head was racing and pounding as the taxi sped to the railway station. But too late; I missed my train by seconds and had to wait a good time for the next. Eventually it came and I bundled in, just hoping I wouldn't miss my flight. In those days, we could check in at the Gloucester Road Terminal in Central London where luggage was weighed and tickets processed. Then a bus would take you to the airport. Arriving at Waterloo, I yelled for a porter who raced me and my suitcases to another taxi. We just about made it to the terminal where the bus was waiting for me. With many apologies, I boarded the bus and off we went to the airport. I was the only passenger!

On arrival at the airport with no time to lose, I was given my seat number and boarded the plane. Phew! Now I could relax but no sooner had I entered the plane than I became aware that something was wrong. What, I didn't know. But I sensed something. Panic wanted to take over. Don't be such an idiot I thought to myself; calm down, and get such stupid thoughts out of your head. Relax! But how could I? The awareness was far too strong to be overlooked and I had no pills to relieve the pounding in my head. I asked the stewardess for an Aspirin which helped reduce the pain. Ironically, due to heavy air traffic, we waited one hour before take off; at exactly 12 noon.

The plane was a turbo jet; I had a window seat over one wing and at 1.15 pm I watched with horror as one of the propellers stopped spinning. This is it, I thought. I was right. I expected the plane to nosedive at any moment and was prepared for panic among the passengers but all I heard was the pilot's voice over the intercom telling us we had engine trouble and were returning to London. At 2.15 pm we were back where we started; Heathrow! Was I glad the man in the travel bureau was not around to witness the return of the Mule. But I didn't need a return ticket for it, did I?

I phoned my sister (Audrey) in London to tell her what had happened. She suggested I spent the night with her but I insisted on going on the next flight. How easily I could have given up there and then, returning to known security; just about everything so far had gone wrong.

At 3.45 pm we took off again, finally reaching Salzburg at 6.10 pm instead of the scheduled 2.30 pm. At the airport information bureau, I asked for a hotel where I could spend a few nights. 'Not too expensive,' I said. The lady wrote down a name on a scrap of paper then I went outside to join the crowds waiting for a taxi. I waited and waited. Suddenly it dawned on me that people didn't queue like they did in England, they just pushed towards the taxis as they arrived; it was first-to-push first served. I was by now the only one left. Back at the airport information bureau, I asked the lady to help by phoning for a taxi. Outside again, I played the waiting game. It was dark and very cold, my clothes were quite inadequate. Finally a taxi came and I got in and showed the driver the hotel name written on the scrap of paper. 'I know of a hotel where you can spend at least three nights for the price this one,' he said. 'Take me there,' I answered, too exhausted to care at this point. All I wanted was to sleep.

The journey was endless, we drove on and on. The city disappeared then fields covered in snow appeared. I was now sure I was being kidnapped but there was nothing I could do about it, I just had to wait. At last we arrived at a place that looked more like a castle than a hotel. Thankful, I paid the taxi driver, and in the hotel was shown a room and a welcome bed.

Quite unknown to me at the time, the Lord had miraculously transported me to the very place that was to be the hub for my entire stay in Austria. From that small centre, all my contacts, work, and living accommodation were to proceed for the next five-and-a-half years. Could my reckoning have been as wonderfully planned as this seemingly reckless ill-fated journey? I leave you to say yea or nay! I know what I would say.

My clothes were not nearly warm enough for the much lower temperature. I had left England in moderate weather but here I was thrown into the depths of winter.

The next day, feeling so much better, I went off early to the city to find a job centre and, in the process, discovered I had only a few days to find work and register with the police. Inquiring about work, I was told a lady had phoned the centre and asked if there was an English person to help her in her house and to speak English with her two children. Nothing goes smoothly like this, I thought to myself, but I took the job as the hotel I had been taken to was being redecorated and they wanted me out for a while. Now I had papers to fill up, names and addresses to give, and a visit to the police to pay a fee of 30 Austrian schillings.

The house I moved into was on a main road in the centre of Salzburg. The front overlooked the street but the back was jammed between houses with no outlook or space at all. My bedroom was tiny, and I had a window looking out to a nearby brick wall. The only light I could see was high up between the roofs of the surrounding houses. Not a basement prison this time but an upstairs prison. It was frightful. I hated going into that room as I became claustrophobic. But, I thought, at least I had a place to live and earn some money for the time being, until I could find something else.

It wasn't long before I discovered that the mother who had hired me had no time for her two children. They were in her way. She had a boyfriend and that seemed to be all she cared about. It was heart-breaking; those poor children would have happily accepted me as their mother had I stayed, they needed so much love and help. But I remained two weeks in all, explaining that I was not prepared to take a mother's place when the proper mother was already there, and whose duty it was to bring up her own children. Oh the joys of growing older, one can speak so much more freely and get away with it. We parted friends, and I returned to the hotel.

Again the search began to find somewhere to live and another job. Asking guidance on both, I set out from the hotel one morning to explore the surroundings.

Oh, the wonder and beauty I beheld! The air was filled with the smell of burning wood from warming fires. The huge stacks of logs, all cut into even lengths and piled up in the most orderly fashion, sheltered and dry under the overhanging roofs from which huge icicles hung. It took me back to those wonderful winters in New York State. Many of the houses had Zimmer Frei notices hanging on outside signs; frei meaning vacant, not free. Passing one house, I was clearly told to go and ring the bell but for some reason I took fright and turned into the gate of the house opposite. You might have thought by now I would have learned to obey immediately. So why didn't I? I just don't know. So I knocked on the door of the house opposite but there was no Zimmer Frei. 'Try the house opposite, she has vacancies,' said the woman at the door. Yes, I'd already been told to go there but why was it I went without hesitation on the command of this lady and not on the Lord's?

What patience the Lord has with his hesitant children. He may not have had problems with the mule He rode for His triumphal entry into Jerusalem but He certainly had problems with this 'she mule' before she made her entry into the bed-and-breakfast lodgings He had chosen for her.

The B&B landlady seemed very nice and I soon met her grandchild. My room was small but adequate with a wash basin. No cooking facilities of course. But it wasn't long before the breakfast disappeared from the B&B; as soon as I found a job, breakfast was only given on my day off. Oh well, I thought, nothing is straightforward or easy on the Turntable.

A few days elapsed when the grandchild asked me if she could show me something. 'Ja,' I replied, whereupon she came eagerly into my room and, to my amazement, opened the draw of my bedside table where I kept a little box of earrings. She fumbled excitedly until she found a pair of blue earrings and then took them out. 'I like these the best,' she said in German. I was dumbfounded but not for long.

'What else do you like?' I asked her, wondering what other of my possessions had been foraged in my absence. She knew where everything was and showed me what her grandmother had also admired. 'Did you find the nice things in my suitcases?' I asked, just wondering if there was anything else that had not been interfered with.

'No,' was the reply, 'there wasn't time!'

I just couldn't believe it. Well, I thought, at least no one had read my letters; no-one except me could speak English in this household. From then on I kept most of my possessions in a locked suitcase. I never complained as I needed that room but I often wondered if the grandmother ever knew her beloved grandchild had let out her deceitful secret.

But now for some work; just up the main road, about 15 minutes walk away, was a large convent school. I was told they might have work. So off I trudged in the snow to make inquiries. Yes, the sister in charge did need help in the cleaning of classrooms and washing up after supper. At first, she was hesitant in employing me for 'this sort of work' but I assured her I was quite used to 'this sort of work' and was taken on.

Austrian-German is different from German-German. I now had a new task of learning new words and soon discovered that my 'hoch Deutsch' was frightfully la-di-da to the hard-working Austrian.

The children at the school boarded from Mondays to Fridays, then went home for the weekends. They brought their own bedding which I thought was a wonderful idea and also had their own cutlery. They ate both courses of their meals from the same plate which were wiped clean, no doubt, with a piece of bread. They weren't the type of children who would lick the platter clean; it just wasn't that kind of a school.

My hours were 12 noon to 8 pm, including meals. More forms had to be filled, letting the authorities know what I had to do and was not loafing around but doing an honest day's work. And let me say, the Austrians worked hard.

On 18 March 1971, I walked up the road from my new home to begin my honest day's work. First, we ate a meal in the workers' staff room. I don't know why the staff found me so amusing but they did; except one girl who appeared to hate me like poison. I was to find out later that she hated the way everyone laughed with me, can you believe it? I soon made friends with a lot of the sisters, especially in the kitchen.

With broom, dustpan and brush, mop, bucket, rags, dusters, polish and elbow grease, I was shown my classrooms. They were vast. Here we go again I thought, still the ruddy job of cleaning up. 'Will it ever end, Lord?' The windows were gigantic, swivelling around until they were back to front, marvellous for leaning. But I was terrified they would swing off their hinges, or whatever they swung on. I must have walked miles in the course of my eight-hour shift. It took me ages to find my way around, eventually finding the rubbish bins outside the huge modern kitchen where three elderly sisters worked all day producing meals for both the children and their own community which I gathered wasn't small. I sank down for supper when the time came; totally worn out. The food was rather starchy and it wasn't long before I had bowel problems. Austrian food is very different from English food, I found.

After our own supper, we helped load food onto trolleys and wheeled them into a huge dining room for the girls. I think they had mostly cold meats and bread. When, finally, silence prevailed, grace was said, then the din recommenced. After the meal was over, the children stacked their plates onto the trolleys, leaving debris in-between. What a sorry sight it was.

We washer-uppers had our own little L-shaped corner of the kitchen. There was a dishwasher but no cup machine, so pride of speed did not enter the convent kitchen. Also we were living, or should I say preparing, for eternity; not time on Earth so speed was not the order of the day. A different sister helped me each evening; I'm sure the slowest of the slow was chosen to teach me patience. So my job was to wipe the things up, then put them away. The girls did their own cutlery and what a difference that made.

Our L-shaped working area heated up like an oven and was periodically enveloped in steam; we had no windows and always had to work with lights on. When the dishwasher was opened, huge racks of plates were rolled onto the draining boards. It was heavy and hot work but no lifting was required. I was fortunate to have precious little on under my overalls but the sisters who helped were in full regalia. Their veils were long, and so were their habits. I turned crimson in the heat; so did the sisters, at least according to the small exposed area of their faces. After work came the lovely walk home in fresh air.

The nuns were such lovely people. Many of them could speak English and I chatted with them in the corridors or in our dining room. The sister-in-charge of the working staff thought it would be nice if I had some German lessons from one of the elderly sisters so I turned up at the convent much earlier than prescribed for my honest day's work. It was marvellous; I started learning the passive voice and the subjunctive case which, incidentally, I still find difficult. Naturally, the lessons were taken from the book of books, *Die Heilige Schrift*.

All went well and I made great progress until one day I almost shocked the elderly sister into the next world by referring to *Die Heilige Schrift* as the Bible. What horror; God's Holy Writ being called by that cheap and nasty modern word – Bible. I was sure my lessons would come to an abrupt end but no; after the shock had subsided, they continued as usual.

I clearly remember two sweet sisters who were always together. Dare I say they appeared to think as thieves? They always came into our dining room to have a chat with us, or rather with me. One especially wanted to learn a few more English 'vords.'

'What say you, when you raise glass?' she asked one day, going through all the actions with an empty tea cup.

'Cheers,' I told her, repeating the action for her benefit with another tea cup. Every time from then on, she would raise her empty hand with an imaginary glass in it saying with a broad grin, 'cheers.' Then I would lift my hand up in reply saying, 'prosit.' Wherever or whenever we met, we greeted each other with the same toast, regardless of what we had in our hands; hers were mostly empty, but mine loaded with the usual cleaning materials. Whatever was in my hand, it went up in celebration, be it a duster, dustpan or brush. It struck me as very funny, in a convent of all places.

I did my best to behave 'proper' while working there, moving about in what I considered an appropriate manner. Running was out, and only quiet respectable talk was the norm; high- pitched laughter was definitely never expected and whistling was nearly my undoing - never, within those Holy walls.

Friday was half-day working but some of the girls stayed for lunch. On arrival, my first task was to deal with a mountain of washing up all by myself before cleaning the classrooms. It really was a depressing sight to see the piles of badly stacked plates with all the uneaten bits sticking out between them. Before washing, there needed to be a massive cleaning operation and rinsing in water. One afternoon, in the midst of it all, the dishwasher running, me banging around, lugging the baskets and plate racks in and out of the machine, I decided my soul needed a boost. I began whistling. The work went on, stacks of dirty crocks diminishing and stacks of clean crocks increasing when, turning round with a large pile of plates in my arms to take into the kitchen. I beheld three veiled heads peering at me around the L-shaped corner of the kitchen. The next 'sin' was about to be committed - I burst out laughing. The sight of the three elderly nuns, listening in horror at the sound that issued from the corner of their kitchen, brought all my daily efforts at being proper crashing down; unheard of within these Holy walls. Never again did I dare show such an outward sign of an inward joy? It was so improper.

Over time, however, I began to notice something strange happening with those three elderly sisters who worked so faithfully within the holy walls of their kitchen; a sneaky little joy was beginning to infiltrate each one of them. They began to walk with a lighter step and their mouths stretched from east to west much more frequently. I spent a lot of time talking with them and even discussed the Holy Writ once with one of them.

One day, I dared tell the youngest of the three (heaven alone knew how old she was) that all was not well with my inside; I needed more fruit and vegetables! The sister had a quick answer: 'The Lord told us to pray "give us each day our daily bread," not fruit and veg.'

'Ah,' I replied, knowing quite a lot of the Holy Writ myself, 'He also said, "thou shalt not live by bread alone ..." ' We never discussed the Holy Writ again.

As soon as I could afford it, I bought myself a suede coat with a hood to wear against the cold which was bitter in winter, and therein laid another amusing story. I had discovered a short cut which saved at least five minutes getting home from work. Part of the short cut took me past a section of the convent building and to ward off the biting cold I would pull up the hood of my coat. One morning I arrived at work to hear there had been considerable panic the previous evening within the convent walls; someone had seen a hooded figure walking past the building and disappear into the night. The ladies panicked. Every room was searched, doors and windows tested for security. One sister told me she was too scared to go to the 'you know where' during the night, in case a man was hiding there. What an uncomfortable night she must have had. They were convinced it had been a wandering monk who had become lost. Because of the timing and the description I could only imaging that it was, in fact, me.

In spite of everything, the hours were long and the work was hard; my legs began to swell from being on them so long and it became apparent that a less strenuous job shold be found. One day, I enquired at a large hotel in the city to see if there was less strenuous work and was offered a job checking clean linen on its return from the laundry. I accepted the job there and then, explaining at the convent my reasons for leaving. They were all very sad to hear I was going but they quite understood. If I hadn't brought open laughter to within those holy walls, I had at least brought smiles, especially to the three elderly nuns in the kitchen.

As the new job involved sitting much of the time, I decided to walk to work. This meant getting up at around 5.15 am and leaving my B&B home punctually 6 am. In that beautiful morning landscape, the air was like wine and, after leaving work at 3 pm, I would walk home along the River Salzach. The walking not only kept me fit but the ever-changing visual scenic beauty of the seasons brought me much inner joy.

How I adored Salzburg. I felt at long last that I belonged somewhere. At the end of each year, I had to fill up a form and pay a fee in order to work and live in Austria for another year. I always wrote the same answer against the question, 'why do you wish to stay?" Answer, 'because I love your country and your people.' It remains so even today. My heart and thoughts are permanently there; I live with an insatiable longing to be among those mountains and that way of life.

Salzburg was where my photography started in a big way. I took my camera around with me, capturing sights and scenery of the four seasons. One of my favourite places was Hellbrun, just outside the city. The gorgeous colour of the buildings, the gardens ablaze with flowers, the trout in the huge ponds, swans on the river, and the wonderful courtyards where one could sit at tables with red and white checked cloths on them under colourful umbrellas, sipping over-strong coffee and eating cake, staying as long as you liked.

During the summer during the Salzburg Festival, the city became packed with visitors. I loved listening to the English-speaking community, swarming about the narrow streets and arcades, admiring this and that. As autumn came, the crowds disappeared again.

All through the winter I continued walking to work. I was still the mad Englishwoman who walked when she could have ridden. Why didn't I catch the colds and flu that took hold of the staff so often? No one could explain. It remained a mystery.

By January 1972, I felt the pressure of guidance to start looking for somewhere else to live. As mentioned earlier, I was not expected to stay all day in my B&B room, even on my day off. Also, I wasn't allowed to have friends visit me, not even a female. If I wanted to chat with a friend, it had to be in a café; once it was in a bus shelter. I was getting rather tired of this and there was really nowhere to go for the day if it was wet and cold. I began to look around for another room but without success. My landlady had become rather off-handed towards me, and many times I returned at what I considered a decent enough hour only to find I was locked out of the house; she had bolted the door from the inside. I rang and rang the doorbell until somebody let me in. At first there were the usual excuses: 'Oh my husband must have bolted the door.' I thought she wanted more money for the room and offered her more but she wouldn't take it. Then I knew she wanted to get rid of me. Why? Your guess is as good as mine but I put it down to the Lord's timing again, something I had to accept.

Once again I felt a ghastly feeling of insecurity although I knew I was not alone. Oh yes, I was given assurances. 'You must rely on Me alone. You must depend on My divine powers. You cannot be anxious if you know that I am your supply.' How wonderful it is to receive words of assurance like that when you're in a difficult situation, but it takes a lot of faith to hold on when you know someone is kicking you out and your search bears no fruit.

It was at this time that a picture came into my mind. It looked like a building or something standing completely on its own; the only thing that was really clear was that the building, or whatever it was, had windows all the way round. Beyond this, I could not see any detail. But a person I'd previously met came clearly into my mind. I knew I must contact her, perhaps she could help. I put the visit off a couple of days but felt the inner persuasion that usually lifted me from my disobedience and laziness. Taking a bus, I paid her a visit but she couldn't help me; the lady lived on the other side of the river and, in all the time I had been in Salzburg, I had never explored that side. While there, I looked around but there were no houses with windows all the way round; it was all very puzzling. Getting on a bus to return home, I passed some caravans for sale in an off-the-road place and immediately felt an inner leap of recognition. They had windows all the way round. Was I at last on the right track?

The next day I returned by bus, getting off near the caravans where a salesman showed me many of the smaller types, then eventually took me to a much larger model that had been turned into an office. As I followed the salesman, my heart thumped and my head raged. The inner voice clearly told me, 'you must buy this.'

'But where on earth, Lord, am I going to put it?' I asked inwardly.

So what was I worrying about? Hadn't my whole life been a bit back to front? Didn't the cart always appear before the horse? Since when had I seen the end before the beginning? How many times had I been told to do something, to go somewhere and the way had opened only after I'd obeyed in faith. I had never known it any other way.

'Launch out into the deep and let down your nets,' the disciples were told with no promise of a catch. They caught nothing at first but were put to the test again. This time they were told exactly which side of their boats they had to let down their nets. The whole point of the story to me was that they obeyed before they had proof of anything else. Even if they did not fully believe what the Lord had told them to do, they went at His command!

Now do you honestly think the Lord would have told me to buy a caravan without knowing there was a place to put it? Certainly not! He just doesn't work like that. The ladder we are asked to climb has a secure base, it is held in eternity by His wonderful hands. The higher rungs may be out of view in the mists of time but they will never become clear until we trust the One who is holding the ladder and climb. Too many people stick around at the bottom or the first rung and refuse to climb because it appears to be going into the unknown. So, with all the impossibilities that appeared to me at that moment, I ordered one of the large caravans. The salesman suggested to me I parked it at a camp site. He knew of one not too far away from where I was living, and did the enquiring for me there and then; 'Yes,' came the answer over the phone, so long as I had my own metre for electricity. The caravan had to come from England so I had to wait awhile. It would also take the very last of my savings. But now I had more to learn about the waiting game.

What a lesson waiting is isn't it? Is it because there's nothing we can do but wait? To my mind, inactivity is always harder than activity. How frustrating it is to do nothing when we have become so accustomed to work and move at high speed. We live in an 'instant' world; instant tea, instant coffee, instant everything. We can't wait and can't stop. Sitting still and standing still have become almost impossible. Have we lost the virtue of patience? Patience with ourselves first, then we shall have patience with others.

I found the patience to await the arrival of my caravan almost intolerable, much of it because I was being pressured by my landlady. She wanted to know when I was leaving, when the caravan was arriving. How could I say when I didn't know myself? The final 'B' of the B&B was now warm coffee with a roll on my day off! Are we not all guilty of this kind of behaviour when we're not getting our own way? Unknown to me, she had already let my room to someone else from a certain future date, hoping that I would be out by then. Little wonder she was so impatient (hateful at times) with me; me who was trying to wait patiently. But wait I had to, I could do nothing else. Time crept on and still nothing happened; no word from either side of the Channel. What should I do if this all this fell through? Where should I go? I started looking at the waves and the storm engulfing me, I began to take my eyes off my 'Captain' who was steering me through these storms on apparent unchartered waters and, like Peter, I began to sink. It was the unknown again that was frightening me; the fear of insecurity, the helpless waiting

On holiday in England, 1972

when I wanted to get going. If only I could do something to remedy the situation. It's one thing to trust and believe when you have reached the safety of the harbour but, out on the high seas of life, it's a very different experience. You must believe there will be a harbour even when it hasn't come into view. In desperation I cried out one morning, 'Oh Lord, please give me some encouragement. Give me word or something to let me know all's well!'

Next morning, as I was dressing, a goods train rumbled down the line towards the city. I had grown used to the trains by now so didn't pay much attention. Casually, I looked through the window and there before my eyes on a wagon was my future home. I almost cried with joy. So it had finally arrived.

On 15 June 1972, I moved out of the room that had been my home for so long into my caravan that had been set up on the camp site, just 10 minutes walk from the first hotel I stayed in on my arrival in Austria. Now I hoped to be able to find another job close by and leave the hotel where I worked, and no sooner had I met the manageress of the site than I was offered work in the camp site Information Bureau. Of course, I accepted it and was able to leave my job at the hotel.

Chapter 10

Imagine a mad English woman moving onto a campsite with a caravan that has no electricity, no toilet or bath, and no running water. The mad woman was, of course, me; not forgetting that I had been clearly told to buy the caravan. For half a year, the Eigen Camping Platz provided most amenities except electricity which I had installed with my own metre. I was connected to a main at a nearby restaurant so could get power all year round; that was unless the old lady who lived in the restaurant inadvertently turned off the switch. But what about the other half of the year, including winter, when campsite amenities were closed? I had wondered how I was to cope with no running water and no toilet but, having been so clearly guided in this venture, I knew I was in the right groove on the Turntable and that every step of the way had been planned. It was then just a matter of facing problems only when and if they appeared.

I bought items such as bedding, pots and pans, a fridge, water carriers, buckets for many different purposes, and other basics, swelling my earthly goods to well beyond the size of two suitcases; but the Lord would know what to do in any further move, wouldn't He?

Solitude at Eigen Camping Platz

It was also essential to insulate my caravan against the winter. Snow lay up to four months each winter in temperatures well below zero. Really, the caravan was only fit to live in during the summer. But how lovely it was to have a place where I could come and go as I pleased. It was interesting that, after I'd left my B&B room, the landlady came to find out all she could about my new home. She was charming. How much did it cost? Did I have work? Was I happy? Sugar-coated words spilled from her once sour mouth. I found it impossible to be more than curtly polite to her. The curiosity I caused was substantial. No one it seemed had seen a caravan as large as mine. It was about 24-feet long and, in the main section at one end, had a stove and sink side by side opposite an eating area, then a recess where I put the fridge; the bedroom was at the other end. There was just enough space for an ordinary length bed with a built-in unit comprising a cupboard, draws, and a mirror. I had a few alterations made to accommodate the plastic water carriers which I had to take inside in winter to prevent the water in them from freezing. A small cupboard was installed for cleaning materials, buckets and such like. To insulate the floor, I bought polystyrene slabs plus glue and glued them into place by sliding underneath the caravan on my back. In doing so, I had the deepest sympathy for Michelangelo when he painted the ceiling in the Sistine Chapel, slung up there on his back.

I also encountered difficulties when starting work at the campsite Information Bureau which, as well as being the site's administration centre, sold souvenirs, gas, batteries, towels, soap, stamps; everything a holiday-maker might need. At the outset, I warned the manageress that my arithmetic was not good but she refused to believe me; until I inadvertently proved I was telling the truth. When dealing with the visitors, I was fine with those who spoke English, of course, and German but a thousand other languages were needed besides.

Visitors were registered on arrival, the few rules and regulations that existed were explained to them, and a number was given to put on tent or caravan, whichever it was, so we knew who was who, but much of this required different languages.

The French arrived with their 'Parlez vous Francais?'

I replied with my usual 'non,' having forgotten almost all French I had learnt at school. But my 'non' made not the slightest difference; they babbled in their own tongue accompanied by the most generous of gestures.

'Lumiere?' they would ask, getting irritated with this woman who was supposed to be the bureau's fountain of information. I hadn't a clue what the word meant but noticed that every time it was used, it was accompanied by a finger pointing heavenward. This puzzled me until I asked the manageress who spoke most languages it seemed.

It means 'Do you have electricity?' she said. Oh, how dim could I be?

I soon learnt that the Belgians spoke different French from the French. Not that I could understand them either, but at least they did attempt to communicate in German. Americans, New Zealanders and Australians expected us to speak their language which fortunately I did. They walked in as if on home territory with a 'Hi there,' or 'good-day' and ignored any possible language barrier. Occasionally there was a 'Sprechen Sie English?'

When I wanted to tease I might reply 'Nein,' not batting an eyelid. The ensuing conversation would sometimes attract compliments on my splendid English. 'Well I did learn in England,' I would say. But in my dirndl, apron and pretty blouse, I always hoped I looked like a fully-fledged Austrian. Only the Austrians weren't deceived.

The scenery around the campsite was magnificent. For hours, I wandered up the mountainsides seeing hardly a soul all day. There were waterfalls, cascading through giant boulders, joining rivers at the base. This source was my main water supply during the winter when the campsite was closed. Fortunately there was guttering around my caravan enabling me to collect rain water in enormous containers but I only drank water from the mountains. To avoid carrying so much, and to save what I collected, I washed my clothes in the caravan, then carried them into the woods to clear pools of water at the base of one of the many waterfalls; this of course was after the camp had closed until re-opening in May. I went very early in the morning when no-one was around. Not having any running water, it was much easier that way. Also, the waterfall pools were much larger than my sink!

Naturally, I preferred not to be seen. I felt I was already regarded as somewhat eccentric and that it would be the last straw if I were seen bending over the pool rinsing my smalls. Mostly I remained unseen except for a few early-morning joggers. I acquired an old pram, discarded the body, and laid a board across the base. On this went my water containers in the winter after I'd filled them from the waterfall, and transported them to my caravan.

I was offered some housework jobs during the winter so that took care of the money situation. They were local jobs and, by that time, I'd bought yet another bicycle in my life, so I could get about more easily. One lady I worked for was a midwife. She gave me the house key as she often didn't come home until late morning. Also in the house were two lovely collie bitches, very well trained. At midday, when I finished work, I took them for a run, me on bicycle, the dogs in tow, along paths that went all around the campsite and surrounding fields. The dogs adored the run; I could never have walked fast enough for them but this way they really had to move to keep up. Half an hour before I finished work, the dogs somehow knew their run was near and they began wagging their tails furiously. When I opened the door to let them out, I was all but knocked over in their rush to get out; and the barking! I took them out most of the year, except when they were on heat when they were not allowed out. At this time, all the neighbours' dogs congregated outside the garden gate and, when it was time for me to leave (on my own), I was obviously permeated with their smell too. Now, with the neighbours' dogs chasing me, I became a kind of Pied Piper; getting home with great difficulty. When I did manage to get inside my caravan, the dogs waited patiently for hours outside my front door, no doubt to return eventually to the garden gate of their would-be suitors. Was I glad when those lovely collies returned to normal?

Costs were minimal during the winter months. I paid no rent when the site was closed, no rates, and certainly no water charges. A plastic waste pipe ran from my sink into the adjacent fields. When the area became waterlogged, I just moved the pipe a foot or so. Life was simple.

Every evening, I wrote up my diary. Of course, people were curious about what I did so I just told them I was a writer. So I was, but not in the way they thought. Still it kept them quiet. I carried a notebook and pencil with me on my walks to jot down anything I wanted to remember and revelled in the beauty around me, taking long walks up the hills and mountains. Then, in the evening, down would all go in detail into my notebook. Here is part of one such account:

> 'Although it is the middle of October, the day is hot and the sun shines in a cloudless sky. It's ten past six in the morning and I watch the sun rise over the mountain tops, flooding them in vivid crimson. The frost lays thick on the fields; the air is crisp and clear. In the distance, the trees with their coloured foliage gradually come to life as the sunlight reveals yellow, gold, scarlet, russet and bronze. The colours stretch for miles across the base of the mountains and valleys. As the sun rises higher, melting the frost, long patterns of white and green weave themselves into odd shapes and designs over the fields until half in sunshine, half in shadow. I start out on my morning walk and, as it is cold, jog along the stony path that lead into the woods, the crisp air stinging my face and my half dead fingers tingling with a new inner warmth.
>
> 'I enter the woods where the sound of gently trickling water reaches my ears. Following the sound, I see a tiny flow of fresh mountain water that the recent snows, already on the highest mountains, have brought. The waterfalls and rivulets that had been silent throughout the summer months are now coming to life again. This fresh water trickles like a jewel set between rounded grey stones, then wanders under the fallen leaves and way out of sight and hearing. I pause to examine a pool of new sparkling water, bending over to cup a little in my hands. It tastes marvellous; ice cold, and so pure. Again I cup my hands to taste more and, as I do so, my eyes fall on the mirrored reflection in the pool, clearer than a looking glass. Golden leaves intermingle with some crimson, rust, brown, lime-green and orange. Beyond this tapestry of colour is the vivid blue sky. So deep is the stirring within me, I want to cry at the wonder of it all.

'The mountains are fantastically detailed in the morning light and I feel I can put out my hand and touch them. Each summit is capped with a spotless white mantle of newly fallen snow. I stand spellbound, looking at a scene that only a Master Hand could have created.

'Below lays the city, fading into the misty horizon. The Schloss, looking so high from the valley, appears like a toy on the hill in comparison to the mountains that surround it. The river meanders through a maze of golden-brown chestnuts that line its path. The many cupolas and spires of the churches reflect gold, silver and bronze under the sun's blaze. A low-lying mist, strung in the valley like a wad of cotton-wool pulls thin at each end. The laughter of the woodpecker echoes through the hills …

'The higher I climbed, the more magnificent becomes the view. Mountains grow bigger, the city smaller, the haze deeper, and the clarity clearer. Taking the path through the grounds of a farmhouse, I notice window-boxes still with pink and white petunias in bloom. The dahlias have not yet been bitten by the frost and happily nod their heads of red, purple, white, yellow and pink. Leaving the farmhouse, I climb even higher until I enter more woods. It's now ten o'clock and the day is warming up; so am I for that matter. The tinkle of cow bells in a field beyond wafts through the air, bringing fairy music through the glade. There is no time here.

'Now the way begins to descend and I become aware of the smell of manure somewhere nearby. Around the corner a farmhouse appears. The misty blue haze of the mountains in the distance makes the whitewashed wall of the farmhouse appear even whiter by contrast. A boy is playing with a tricycle but he doesn't notice me; three kittens play in a wooden box. I go over to join in their fun but two run away, the third looks very frightened when I stroke it. Here at the farmhouse, I meet the only person on my entire day's outing - a man, no doubt out to look and listen like I am. 'Gruss Gott,' (literally 'Greet God') we both greet each other; then continue our separate ways.

'Descending through more fields, I came across a stone carved head of a man wearing a hat. The hat is full of weeds but out of the pipe he is smoking comes a jet of mountain water falling into a tiny trough under his chin; beside him is a tin mug chained to the wall. I have to laugh. The stone man looks so comic there in the middle of nowhere but his water tasts good.

'As the sun creeps lower, the roofs of the wooden huts light up like golden tiles. The sight lasts all but moments then, quite suddenly, the night puts her arms around the sunset, and draws it under her cloak, leaving me sitting on the hill, staring into a colourless landscape.'

During winter when the campsite was closed, I was quite alone. The house where the manageress lived was in view but not close. Occasionally, a passing visitor parked his caravan nearby. I have never understood why people herd together when there is so much space. Could it be fear? However, every latecomer chose to park his caravan very close to mine. This infuriated me. After all the noise during the season I loved the solitariness of the winters, and didn't want to hear human sounds. I'm sure somebody will think this mean and unchristian, but I revel in silence. Over the course of time, I discovered ways of removing these visitors; it was very simple, I just started singing scales. Up and down I screeched (behind drawn curtains of course), first on ah's, then on me's and oo's etc. The din was awful. Even the cat I had at that time shook its ears. The desired effect took place in about ten minutes. Soon, I heard clink clank, then an engine, and soon, the newly arrived visitor was driving off as far away from me as possible. Naturally, when the visitors had removed themselves, I saw no reason to continue my voice production, and my cat went back to sleep.

With the reflection of the snow, the nights were never dark. I would wake during the night to hear the sound of falling snow, so great was the silence. I had no fear living there alone, and experienced no trouble either. Sometimes, I would watch huge hares playing in the snow. It was the most wonderful sight. They leapt into the air, chasing each other round in circles. Then they stood on their hind legs and boxed each other. Suddenly, they would dash off to continue their game further away. I also had the fabulous view of herds of deer crossing the fields, passing close to my caravan. In the rutting season, one enormous male would shatter the night with its amazing barking call. Its voice echoed around the hills while the herd made its way across the white fields in bright moonlight.

1976 in Salzburg

One winter, I fed a male pheasant that found the seed I put out for the birds. Although it was used to seeing me through the window, it ran away if I dared move. Never have I seen such a variety of birds that came to my bird bar which was hung just outside the caravan. Nuthatches and greenfinches were the most numerous; then came all kinds of tits, bullfinches and a pair of hawfinches. There were redstarts, and black redstarts, thrushes, blackbirds and sparrows. They didn't sing in Austria like they did in England, except in the dawn chorus. In summer, I would get up any time after four o'clock, and sit outside my caravan with a cup of coffee listening to the dawn chorus. The fields were yellow with dandelions and buttercups, and the scent exquisite.

Twice only in this crazy way of life did I think I might die. The first time was from flu. I went down with it in winter, in the early hours of the morning. I ached from head to foot, and couldn't get warm. I used everything I had on my bed to try and get some body heat going, but all to no avail. Every hour or so, I'd get out to boil water for a hot water bottle, and drink a bowl of soup. Having no phone, I couldn't contact anyone, and this time no one came near. I had no choice but to lay it out. After 24 hours I began to get warm again. The lady I worked for wondered why I hadn't turned up for work, but never thought to inquire if anything was wrong.

In the second experience, again in mid-winter, the temperature one night dropped to minus 10 deg. My electric radiator was on but, even so, it was very cold indoors. Putting on a coat over my night things, I went to light the gas fire and stove to make a cup of coffee but nothing happened. Soon I noticed I was getting much colder very quickly, and knew there was only one thing I could do. So I dressed as fast as I could, knowing I had to get out and move. I pulled on what clothes I could, my hands were so stiff. Throwing on a thick coat and snow boots, I went outside and tried to run, but my body just wouldn't move easily. I walked and walked, until some kind of warmth began to creep back into me. Eventually, my body warmed enough to jog the remaining distance home. Later in the day, the gas cylinders worked as normal. From then on I had a greater understanding for older people when they say they are cold. Luckily, I was able to get out and move which undoubtedly saved the situation. Except for those two occasions, I remained wonderfully healthy during my entire stay in that caravan.

Four months after I'd moved onto the campsite, I was at the Information Bureau as usual when an American came in to buy something and amazed me when he said he was a Baptist minister living just down the road, not five minutes away. He told me of an English-speaking community gathering every Sunday at a Baptist church. I could hardly believe it; a church where I could go every Sunday again. I was about to fly back to England for a week or so, to go to my niece's (Pamela Moffat) 21st birthday party in London, so I promised to contact him on my return. This I did, and began going regularly to the English services that followed the German services at the church. After a while, I also attended the German services. I cannot describe the great emotion I experienced every Sunday at those German services. So great was this emotion, I couldn't sing without my eyes filling with tears. Somehow, I felt I'd come home to my own people in that church.

The English congregation was comprised mostly of Americans with lots of youth. They were warm and friendly people. Marilyn who played the piano was an excellent pianist-accompanist and her improvisation of the hymns and choruses was inspirational. Hearing her play took me back to my early musical training on piano, organ and singing, now almost forgotten. When I knew Marilyn better, I shared with her some of the thoughts that were passing through my mind. One day when I told her about my past, my conversion, and the door finally closing to a hopeful singing career she replied with what I considered to be an amazing thought. 'Have you ever given your gifts back to the Lord, in case He wants to use them?'

Never before had I considered offering back something I knew I had been given in the first place; weren't all these gifts the Lord's anyway? Why, then, was it necessary to offer them back? 'No,' I answered. 'The door so clearly closed, I've never given it another thought.'

A return to the idea of singing had never entered my head. In fact, it no longer mattered to me whether I sang or not, so great was the change that had taken place in me. Many years later, I asked the Lord why He'd closed the door on this career I so longed to have. His answer shattered me. 'You wanted all the glory.' How true His words were. I did want all the glory.

That night at home, however, I did what Marilyn suggested and just before going to bed, I raised my hands up, as though holding the gifts in them saying, 'Well Lord, here they are if You want to use them again, but I don't mind if You don't.'

Some days later, Marilyn invited me and a group of Americans to her home where I was persuaded to air my vocal chords; not, I might add, as I did on the campsite when I wanted to remove unwanted guests. But never had I heard the like. To me it sounded like a voice in a London fog wrapped in cotton wool. Barely had I sung a few minutes when the fog closed right down, throwing a blanket over the vocal chords altogether. I just gave up. Marilyn however, must have heard differently and was thrilled but as far as I was concerned the voice could stay in the London fog forever.

Returning home later by bus, I became aware of a growing inner excitement and anticipation that something wonderful was about to happen. By the time I got off the bus, this excitement had reached fever pitch. I skipped and jumped along the dark lane in exhilaration. But what was it that was about to happen? I had no idea but so great was the joy inside me, I couldn't sleep; certainly not until sometime after the chimes of the local church struck midnight, and then at 5 am I was wide awake again, feeling an ecstasy that whatever was going to happen was imminent. That inner voice spoke to me: 'You are going to sing again, and write your own music.' Leaping out of bed, I began to sing and this time I heard the most glorious voice. It was not my previous voice resulting from years of training but a new, different voice. I couldn't understand it. After all those years I had been told I was going to sing again. The elusive gift that had broken my heart so long ago was now being given back as it were. This time, there were no thoughts of wanting glory.

Visits from the family, here from sister Barbara and husband

There had been no mistaking the inner voice either, or the words that had been spoken. Once you have tuned into this voice that speaks so clearly to your heart, you can never fail to recognise it when it speaks again. For me, it comes with a great uplifting power, taking me up, out and beyond place and time. I was being made aware of the approach of these things in advance; and why shouldn't the Lord share His thoughts and plans with His children in advance? We are heirs of God, and joint heirs with Christ. What a position, what an inheritance; passed down from Father to Son, and from Son to His children; ours by right because of our 'right relationship' with our heavenly Father. We are inheritors of His Kingdom; all that He has is ours for the asking, not because of anything we have done but because of our relationship with God the Father. Surely He must love to share Himself with His children?

What was I expected to do now; start training again and, if so, with whom? Perhaps I had to wait, I didn't know. I phoned a musical lady I'd met some months previously and asked if she knew of a singing teacher. Yes, she did; and she gave me the name and address of a Frau Meyer. Before making contact, I prayed that I was not about to make a mistake; it certainly seemed the right thing to start singing lessons again, and soon I was starting lessons with my fourth teacher.

I studied with this lovely lady for about nine months. She was kindness itself; making copies of music I could not afford. Actually, I couldn't afford the lessons either, they drained my finances drastically. It was while in such a sorry financial state that the Lord gave me another delightful experience of His constant provision for us His children. In addition to the cost of the singing lessons, another expense popped up; a government fee of 30 Austrian Schillings for my application to stay in Austria another year. At the time, I simple did not have the money. I could have borrowed it, I suppose, but I chose to trust that the Lord would somehow provide by the next day which was the deadline for registration and payment.

It was Sunday, my day off from the Information Bureau and I was sitting outside my caravan in the sunshine, thinking about the 30 Schillings I didn't have. Suddenly, the manageress came running toward me. 'Shirley,' she said, 'could you cover for me in the bureau, my little boy has fallen down and cut his head, I must take him to hospital.' I raced to the shop while the manageress drove off to hospital with her child. She returned in exactly one hour. Thanking me very much for helping her in the emergency, she rang up the cash register and took out - yes, exactly 30 Austrian Schillings!

As the months progressed, however, I became disillusioned with my singing. There was this lovely voice I'd heard that morning in the caravan but it was certainly avoiding me now, and with the heavy cost of the lessons I began to think it wasn't worth it. Had I made a mistake? If not, why wasn't this lovely voice showing itself?

It was around this time that I started going to the German services in the Baptist church. It didn't take me long to learn the hymn tunes and soon I was singing lustily with the rest of the congregation, even if I couldn't understand all that I was singing. After one of the services, I was introduced to a 'blind' lady. I put blind in inverted commas as later I discovered she had better sight than many of us. On the day we first met, she told me, 'I can help you with your singing if you wish.'

'Now what Lord,' I asked. 'I've had four teachers in my life, and now a fifth is offering. I'm so fed up by the whole experience; I'm ready to give it all up. Anyway, it doesn't matter to me any longer.'

It was about this time that Frau Meyer's annual concert was coming up, and I was performing. The concert was going to be recorded, so I looked forward to sitting back afterwards and listening to my performance. After the concert I played back the tape and, sheer despair; it was the same old voice I'd always had, with just a variation in tone that different teachers produce. It was definitely not that lovely voice I'd heard and hoped for. I dropped into a pit of despondency and told my Frau Meyer there would be no more lessons. I felt terrible doing this after all her kindness but returned all the music she had lent me and walked out of her house for the last time. On arriving home, I lay on my bed and cried like a baby!

I've often wondered why we both had to go through all that. Wouldn't it have saved a lot of pain and heartache had it never happened? One day, no doubt, we will know the reason but, until then, life seems content to present so many unanswerable questions as if the Lord is asking us to trust Him through a mass of spiritual confusion. Are the tears, the pain and heartache we go through ultimately bringing us into deeper communion with Him?

It was quite some time before I went to the blind lady for lessons, as my will was adamant. I had refused to consider His will for a while but, also on my inner screen, there began to appear other matters that drew out the decision even longer.

I can't recall the exact time of the year when I clearly saw an open space where my caravan stood. But it was quite obvious to me that at some future date it would no longer be there. I should have started to think that another move was ahead but my only reaction was: 'How odd to see an open space where my caravan now stands.' I had lived in it for more than three years.

My sister Audrey had been staying with me and I decided to return with her by train to England for a short holiday. It was May 1975 and I remained in England longer than expected but it was while I was there that I received a letter from the campsite manageress together with an eviction order from the Austrian powers that be. So that was it. The Lord had shown me in advance that a move was to take place but I had failed to recognise it and make preparations.

I felt the eviction was the result of pettiness and not altogether due to the fact that I was no longer employed on the campsite. Perhaps it was due to my having set up a permanent home there. I knew of many other people who would liked to have set up as I had, if only to get away from the noise in the city. And being a foreigner, I would have aroused greater controversy; if others weren't allowed to have permanent caravans on the site, why should she, a foreigner? I couldn't blame their thinking if that is what it was.

Back I flew to Austria in a hurry, wondering what to do. I had one month to get the caravan moved, and I wasn't allowed to place it on any other caravan site either. As usual, the timing and the turn on the Turntable was all in order. I need not have worried.

At the Baptist church, I'd met an Austrian minister, Peter, who worked with the young. I turned to him and, of course, he was the very man I was meant to turn to. He was quick in offering to buy my caravan, as he was planning to set up a Christian Camp and needed somewhere to put up missionaries who were passing through. My caravan was just the right size; big enough. Peter, being an Austrian, had no problem with it up on the campsite. We decided on a price and eventually the caravan was towed away. I was sad, and yet not sad; it had been superb but very tough living. On the day I'd moved in, I told the Lord it was His house to do with as He wished so when the parting came there was no feeling of loss. It had served the purpose for which He had wanted it in my life, and now

He had another purpose for it. I'm sure all those who pass through it are blessed (I'm truly blessed that possessions don't possess me).

I had no doubt as to where I was to go next. Once or twice I'd been to a conference held at a Christian centre some way out of Salzburg; I knew I had to go there. Taking everything I owned from the caravan, and leaving the people for whom I did housework, I embarked on the next groove on the ever-turning Turntable. As I was going to live much further out of the city, I arranged to take less for the caravan on condition that Peter would buy me a moped. I needed some form of transport, especially as I had now decided to take singing lessons from the 'blind' lady, Frau Wiese.

The Christian centre was a long way from the city. To get there, one had to turn off the main road to Grossgmain, climb a long, steady incline, and then descend again into a valley. The only entrance to the centre was along a narrow stony driveway. The centre had once been a mill so there was a river running alongside it in extensive grounds, and naturally the scenery was spectacular. A section of the grounds had been fenced off to keep out marauding animals, and inside was a vegetable garden. I was in my element when I worked there. With a scarf tied around my head, dress and apron, boots and rubber gloves, I tended the garden whenever I could. There was also housework to be done, plus preparation for meals.

The fields were covered with flowers with blooms that were twice the normal size, no doubt due to all the manure that was sprayed on them. Hundreds of butterflies flitted among the flowers. Many I hadn't seen before. Also, there were brightly coloured insects such as beetles. In summer, I would lie on my back gazing up between the flowers and grasses, nearly always displayed against a brilliant blue sky. I had secret hideouts all over the place for all seasons. Sometimes I took my knitting with me and sat against a tree, or on the dry grass, just looking, listening and absorbing. The silence was golden. There were woods covered with dwarf cyclamen, hepatica growing like wild violets low on the ground among dead leaves and melting snows. In autumn, my favourite season, the leaves turned vivid colours. The air was crystal clear, revealing fine details in the mountains which looked close enough to touch them. Swirling early morning mists streaked past as if smoke drifting from a vast fire.

Groups of young people from many countries came with a leader for a few days at the centre; to study, sing, walk, hike, climb, ski, or just meditate in the wonderful scenery and solitude that surrounded the house and grounds. It was while I was at the centre that I began to question many things I was seeing and hearing. All the young visitors had the same 'thing.' But what was that 'thing?' I couldn't figure it out. For the first time in my life I heard them singing in 'tongues.' I'd never had any teaching on this subject, so it came to me as completely new. I would watch the young visitors getting all worked up. Up would go their arms, swaying in unison, clapping while they sang in harmony but I couldn't understand a word they said. They seemed to get lost, but where did they lose themselves? There was an ecstasy attached to it and they appeared to be in another world. What I did know was that I wanted what they had. If this 'thing' would deepen my relationship and communion with my Lord, then I would openly ask to receive it. I asked there and then to receive it.

I travelled by moped to singing lessons with Frau Wiese and feel compelled to recall some of the frolics and falls me and my moped experienced during our year of getting to know each other. There were no rules at the time about wearing crash helmets so I enjoyed the glorious freedom of the warm and sometimes cold air blowing through my hair as I rode. As I didn't weigh too much, I seldom had to pedal to help climb a hill but when I did I had to pedal for dear life. On the whole, the moped proved faithful but it did enjoy a joke or two at my expense. Its main joke was leaving me high and dry in the worst possible places and situations. I had no way of telling when petrol was getting low as there was no fuel gauge. It took me months before I knew how many kilometres I could travel on a full tank, mostly because I invariably forgot to note my mileage before setting out. So I suppose I couldn't entirely blame the moped. However, it usually did the dirty on me when I was on a mountainous climb.

There was about one litre of reserve fuel which I could switch to but that never worked going up hill. Clearly, when the moped was slanting backwards, the petrol couldn't flow forwards. There was only one thing to do. I had to reverse, coast down the hill, until the engine started again then, reversing yet again, I was able to continue my journey just hoping I could make it home before the reserve ran out. This action probably looked crazy but it was the only way I could keep moving. I didn't mind this antic when no-one was around but that rarely seemed to be the case. One day, I was on my way up a long mountainous road, enjoying whistles and catcalls from a group of marching soldiers when my orange Puch decided that this was the moment to stall on its owner. Reversing, I coasted back down the hill, to more whistles and catcalls, feeling just slightly embarrassed; well, imagine their reaction when this moped woman passed them for the third time within a few minutes, peddling for dear life to make the final part of the steep hill. It was at times like these that I could have physically abused my moped. How could it be so inconsiderate?

Whichever way I wanted to go into Salzburg from the Christian centre, I had to ride under the runway of the local airport. The tunnel was always well lit but traffic zoomed through making a deafening noise. I rather enjoyed riding through, with my eyes glued on the tiny hole of daylight the other end growing ever bigger, until finally I whizzed out into daylight again. Every journey passed without incident until, with the approach of winter, I added a windscreen to the moped for protection. On one of my numerous journeys, this time with the windscreen up, a large truck overtook me in the tunnel at high speed. As it passed, I was caught in a violent suction of air which hurled me along at great speed. Narrowly missing the side of the road, there was nothing I could do but sit tight and hope nothing worse would happen. When I finally made the exit, I was shaking like a jelly. Otherwise, I had a couple of nasty falls; one of them was on black ice. It happened just as I was turning to go up the final long hill towards the Christian centre. I skidded into the middle of the road, crashing onto my left shoulder with the moped on top of me.

My moped, though, was how I travelled to visit Frau Wiese, my fifth singing teacher. She was a radiant Christian and, although I was told she couldn't see, her face shone, she moved about her home with the ease of a sighted person, and played the piano well.

At first I could hardly utter a sound without correction. 'You must not raise your shoulders when you take a breath.' How did she see that, I wondered? My jaw was stiff, she said. It was nothing to have her stand behind me, with one of her knees in my back, an arm around my waist, a couple of dozen fingers in my mouth (or so it felt) to flatten my tongue, and somehow she managed to find another limb to pull my chin back until I thought it would be dislocated. 'You must relax!' she said. Relax? How could I relax when every part of my body was being pushed, pulled or pressed into all different shapes and angles? Then she would softly sing a note in my ear. 'Now sing this note.' Somehow I managed to find breath to sing the note and, lo and behold, the most beautiful sound came out. Sometimes my head would be gently swayed from side to side to relax my throat, or straightened if it had gone on the slant. In a very short space of time my voice, which had always been high and brilliant in tone, was now becoming mellow and beautiful. A lower register that I'd never had before was growing and in no time I began hearing the voice I'd heard in my caravan that exhilarating morning. It was indeed a new voice!

As I struggled on, also with the language, my faith and hopes were gradually raised again. I had to learn to get out of old habits; never an easy thing to do. As usual, I practised where and when I could, mostly in the woods and fields. I had sixty-two lessons in all with this 'blind' lady; not many really, seeing I had so much to unlearn. But during that time, Frau Wiese had unknowingly bestowed in me the lovely tone I had waited for from my first teacher. For the first time, I knew my singing voice was beginning to glitter.

Then the door closed yet again.

It was June 1976 and I had been working at the Christian centre for eight months when I became aware that another change was going to take place; again, I had no idea about what or when, it was just something on my inner screen.

Mummy, who was now in her 80s, had moved from Bexhill to Hythe in Kent to be nearer my sister, Barbara, and her husband, Ralph. Many years ago, I had mentioned that, if ever I was needed to help look after her at any time, I would go back. So I wrote to my sister asking if she thought I should now return to England. Her reply said that she didn't think it was time to return. But, as I read her letter, the Lord clearly told me to start preparing to go back. Inwardly, I was very sad about this, I definitely did not want to return but I had made a promise.

My mother was furious when I informed her of my plan. What a fool I was. What with the housing problem in England and no jobs to be had, 'I shall ask God to put some common sense into you,' she wrote in answer to my saying that I had been clearly told to return. Mummy also added that the spare bedroom in her new flat was much too small for a long stay.

Although, I might have been deemed foolish, I was not foolish enough to see I wasn't really wanted. But the Lord had spoken and I'd spoken every Sunday for years, 'send me out as a living sacrifice ...' and a sacrifice it was, to leave the country of my heart. It's like parting from the one you love only this time it was a country. You never quite get over it.

Now the question arose; how was I to return? Soon after my arrival at the centre, it had been made clear that I wasn't to accept any payment in return for my work. It was voluntary anyway, but occasionally a gift of money was offered. The Lord said I was not to accept any. I did a little typing for an American missionary so that was the only income I had during those eight months, except for payments received for the sale of my caravan. As always, my bank balance was low. 'Lord' I said, 'if You want me back in England, please keep me listening in, so that I don't miss Your guidance.' Keeping on with my daily work, I concentrated on extra listening. I didn't have long to wait.

One afternoon, I set out to see the wife of the American missionary I typed for. I wanted to share with her all that was happening. Shep had become a friend but lived a long way away. Even so, the day was wonderful so after lunch I set out on my old pal the moped. The road led through woods, along the side of a mountain that rose on one side, and fell steeply on the other. I remember that wild flowers were in bloom, birds were singing, and the wind in the pine trees brought music to my ears. How lovely it all was. I drove between cornfields and into a valley where there was a picturesque village with a stream flowing through. Cable car cables hung loosely above me, appearing so inadequate to carry the weight of their cars and passengers.

At a crossroads, I needed to turn right to visit Shep but why was I turning left? 'This isn't the way,' I shouted aloud. 'What are you doing? You should have turned right!' As crazy as this may sound, I found it impossible to stop, and continued in the wrong direction, occasionally yelling at myself, 'you're mad, you're completely mad!' I had always thought my moped had a mind of its own and, until today, I'd never hesitated to let it know that I was the boss. But today, I seemed to have no power to stop and turn around; I just drove on and soon came to the lovely village of Anif where Edna, another missionary friend, lived. Oh well, I thought, as I'm here I may as well call in to see her. Yes, she was in and I have to confess I was rather grumpy; I hadn't planned to come this way and my total inability to turn correctly at the crossroads astounded and infuriated me.

Edna, being a mature Christian, decided I needed a walk to cool down; so we stepped into the beautiful scenery and I'm sure she was still patiently hearing me out when she suddenly changed the subject. 'Do you remember the car Johanna bought from Herr Meister?'

'Yes,' I answered, having been stopped mid-flow.

'Well, he has another for sale. He wants the garage space, so it's going cheap.' The remark hit me like a thunderbolt. Immediately in my heart I knew I had to buy that car, even before I had seen it, or inquired how much Herr Meister wanted for it, or whether I could afford it.

So there had been another boss over both me and my moped that afternoon, I thought. Little wonder He had turned me from what would have been the 'wrong' direction to take the 'right' direction. So strong was His guiding hand upon me that I was not able to make a mistake; but also so strong was my desire to know His will in this matter. It was a partnership, Him and me. My wrong turn at the crossroads was right after all and the timing was right too. We were together in the groove, travelling in the same direction.

After learning of the car for sale, we walked to Herr Meister's house. There stood a red Mini Camper with doors at the back. So I was to take my earthly possessions with me. They would all fit in nicely. 'I'll buy the car,' I said to Herr Meister.

'But don't you want to see the engine?' he asked in surprise.

'What do I know about engines even if you show me?' I said. Nevertheless he did show me the engine and, of course, I was none the wiser. Why would I need to look at the engine, I thought? If the Lord has told me to buy the car, would He let me buy a dud that would break down on the way? Is that the way He works? Would He ask me to climb a ladder of faith with faulty rungs, whose base was insecure? Never! He doesn't work like that, and I was prepared to take Him at His word. 'I'll return tomorrow with the money,' I said.

Back at the Christian centre I related my story with excitement but I felt people there weren't sharing my enthusiasm. In fact, I was about to enter one of the most prolonged tests of faith.

The next day I went to the bank to find I just had enough money to buy the car, as my minister friend, Peter, who was buying the caravan from me had just deposited some money in my account. Still on cloud nine, I rode to Herr Meister and paid for the car, about £100, I recall. Later that week, he drove it for me to the Christian centre as it had been years since I'd driven. Also I still had my British driving licence but that was useless in Austria. It was at about this point that I began to think about all that lay before me and I began to slide off cloud nine with astonishing speed.

Suddenly I had around me plenty of well-meaning friends who, although they would not tell me directly, certainly implied they thought I was daft. 'But you didn't have the car vetted,' said the first.

'I would have come and looked it over for you,' said the second. Actually, I thought the Lord had looked over the car, but that seemed to be beside the point and only my opinion.

'You can't drive in Austria on your British licence,' said the third.

'How are you going to get your bicycle in the car; it won't fit,' said yet another. Already a pit was developing in my stomach over what I'd done. Oh well, I thought, I've been a fool for Christ so often in the sight of men, and He's never let me down. I'm quite prepared to be a fool again for Him.

That week, my Mini went for a check-up. The ignition light didn't go off when the engine was running. The brakes needed new shoes. The radiator leaked. My negative friends had been right after all; but I still refused to listen, clinging to my certain proof that the Lord had clearly told me to buy the car. For my part, I told Him I would trust Him, I would believe. He had done the impossible for me up until now and I expected Him to keep doing it. When the bill came for the repairs I again found there was just enough money in the bank as by this time Peter had made another payment for my caravan. I had an offer for my typewriter too which paid for other needs as they arose.

A letter to the authorities in England asked if they would register the car, but they wouldn't, so I registered it in Austria. Soon new licence plates arrived; the old plates had to be sent back on the car's sale. As I intended to take my bicycle with me and, knowing it could only go on the roof, I now needed a roof rack. Somebody had one, but it only half-covered the roof. 'Lord, I need another please!' Sure enough, someone else had one in their garage, and it matched the first. 'Thanks Lord for the pair!'

I watched the journey's preparation with wonder, if with some trepidation. Everything was falling into place but as well as not driving for years, I had never driven with the gear change on the right and I couldn't get any practice except in the grounds of the Christian centre as I had no Austrian driving licence which would allow me to drive on public roads. Also I (or rather He) was planning a journey from Salzburg to the Belgium channel port of Ostend; all on my own. 'Oh Lord, please send me a companion for this journey. You've asked me to step out so often in so many ways, but never before have I undertaken such a giant step in faith like this. Please may I not have to do it on my own.'

A week before I set off, I still had no money for the journey. I had not planned for stopovers, nor did I have a ticket for the sea crossing to Dover. I finished singing lessons and said goodbye to my dear 'blind' teacher Frau Wiese who had transformed my singing voice. I was very sad at the parting but by now so many doors had opened and closed that

I just accepted it as part of life on the Turntable.

I shared what I was about to do with the last group of young people who had come to the Christian centre. If I had already witnessed miracles over provision for the car plus extras, I was about to witness another. To my amazement, money started pouring in. All that week, people put money into my hands. Ten marks, five-twenty marks were pressed into my hands with the Lord's blessing. In the three days before I left, I had acquired quite a sum, about 150 Deutschmarks. This was incredible as at no time had I mentioned my stricken financial state to anyone.

The day finally arrived to pack my belongings into the Mini. There was bedding, clothing, saucepans, a frying-pan, cutlery, a cuckoo clock which, although I stuffed it with a rag, still gave out wheezy jingles and musical jangles. I loaded books acquired over the years onto the front seat, an ironing board somehow fitted lengthwise between the two front seats. Seeing I'd prayed for a companion, I hadn't left much room for one.

The Mini was seriously overloaded, and sagged dangerously at the back, I was told by the husband of a friend who drove my car from the Christian centre to their place where I planned to spend my last night in Austria. And the question of the leaking radiator came up. I began to wonder if I would make the journey.

But then some good news; that evening, I heard that Shep and her husband, the American missionary I had done typing for, were driving to Augsberg. Shep would come with me in the Mini that far. Was this the companion I'd asked for? So faithless me removed the pile of books from the front passenger seat to make room. At least I'd have a companion for the first part of the journey until I became used to the car.

The great day of departure arrived, and I was a wreck. With Shep, my dear friend, at the wheel, we set off until reaching the border area before entering Germany, where she handed the car over to me. The border guards gave Shep a wave; they knew her as she took her children to school in Germany every day. But I was sick with nerves; my head banged, every heart beat brought pain, I was hot and wet through from nervousness.

Shep talked in her quiet manner, encouraging me and keeping my mind off myself and my worries. Gradually, I became used to the car and gained in confidence. We spent the first night in Germany with her friends, and then next day she drove me to the YWAM (Youth with a Mission) Centre at Hurlach where I planned to spend a few nights – and what would I have given to have remained there; the thought of crossing Europe filled me with dread.

At the YWAM, I was given a bed in a room that would be wanted sooner or later for someone else. 'That's all right,' I said, 'I shall then know the exact day I'm to move on again.' Like everyone else there, I gave my services free and helped where help was needed. Immediately I began to notice that the young people around me also had the same 'thing' all the groups of young people had at the Christian centre and it became even more apparent that I didn't have it. Again, I asked to be given whatever it was.

I had been at the YWAM about a week and dearly wanted to stay. Then one morning when I woke up, I knew the Lord was telling me to start the journey again. It seemed miraculous; there wasn't an anxious thought in me, no nervous headache, no fear; I was calm, cool and collected. I was astounded that such a state was possible after all I had been through. That day, I felt I'd been driving long journeys all my life and this was just another undertaking and it wasn't long before my early morning notion was confirmed. On my way downstairs, I met the centre's person in charge as she came to see me. I knew what she was about to say; she needed the room, I had to get going.

I started the engine of my Mini with all the peace and confidence in the world. The cuckoo clock started its wheezes and weird tones in the back of the car. Saucepans under my seat made their own music; just about everything except me had the jitters. With four snow tyres plus my bike lashed on the roof and me in a strawberry coloured Austrian dress, I brought smiles and waves from many a truck driver on this miraculous and stupendous journey that was just beginning.

And I had barely pulled out from the driveway at Hurlach when, on the seat beside me, I saw what must have been an angel! If it wasn't an angel, I don't know how else to describe it. It was a heavenly being. The glory and radiance from its presence filled the entire car and I felt glorified by it. It had no shape or form, neither could it be seen with human eyes but in my inner sight it was clearly beside me on the right hand side where the books were once again piled. Having already thanked God for my friend as a companion, never, never, did I dream of a companion such as this. I sang and laughed and spoke to this wonderful 'being' with exuberance and elation. Even the cuckoo clock, saucepans, cutlery and everything I thought I'd packed so well seemed to jump for joy as we chugged along the autobahn.

But it wasn't all smooth driving. Because my poor Mini was so overloaded, I could only keep in the slow lane where in front and behind me huge trucks and trailers with their drivers towered in their cabs above me. On the inclines, these heavy vehicles were even slower than I was, so I was compelled to follow them in second or, at times, in first gear. However, on the flat they gained speed, overtaking me with waves, grins and shouts, at the diminutive spectacle beneath them.

My first test came on one of the painfully slow inclines. I was locked in between an endless line of trucks with no way out and watched with horror as the temperature gauge on the dashboard went into the red. Remembering the report of a leaking radiator, I thought of hideous consequences and, despite shame that my trust and faith was so small, I cried aloud to this ethereal 'being' beside me. What should I do? I pulled off the road at the next exit and waited half an hour in a lay-by for the engine to cool. Should I turn back? Should I abandon the journey? Fear seized me as I sat waiting but I knew I had to go on; I'd been told to return to England, hadn't I? Starting off again, I eased toward the continuous stream of autobahn traffic and was on my way, in a sweat of nerves. It wasn't long before I saw the temperature gauge rising again and going into the red and, as it did so, I yelled out for help again to the 'being' beside me. Almost immediately and in amazement I watched as the temperature gauge needle began to fall back where it stayed even though I was driving uphill. Now I just had to believe I was in very safe hands. The Mini never overheated again, the radiator never leaked and, as I crossed Germany onto flatter land, the little car sped on with ease with its human and heavenly occupants toward a night stop at Darmstadt.

The next morning I set off once more, my companion still beside me, heading for Ostend and then to cross the English Channel to Dover. The land became so flat that I could see for miles, and a tank of petrol seemed to take us a long way too, much further than on the hilly terrain behind us, but I needed to fill up and pulled in at the next gas station. Funds by now were very low and my inner voice told me, 'only half fill the tank!'

'Half fill the tank?' I answered aloud, 'but You know as well as I do that half a tank will never get us to Ostend.' It's hard to believe that, after all I had previously experienced, I was prepared to query and argue. However, I obeyed and only half-filled the tank. On we went across the flat terrain then, just as I thought, we were again running low on petrol. Again the inner voice spoke, 'Only half fill the tank.'

'But I don't understand,' I queried. 'Had I filled the tank the last time, I would not be stopping again.'

'You will run out of money if you do,' said the voice. I felt a jolt of reality. So that was it; I knew I was getting low on funds but only He knew just how much was needed to complete the journey. Once again I obeyed and half filled the tank.

It was evening when we reached Ostend and the town was a madhouse of people and cars that were everywhere and when I eventually found a parking place, it was under a No Parking sign. Locking the car, I hurried to the cross-Channel ferry office information bureau to inquire about a ticket to Dover. But then, unbelievably, I heard the voice again, 'You're two pounds short, and you're illegally parked. You'd better move quickly before the police find you.'

I ran back to my Mini and, starting the engine, banged on the steering wheel with my fists shouting, 'I don't and won't believe it Lord! You couldn't have brought me all this way to abandon me here without enough money to cross the Channel. What are You going to do about it?' Marvellous isn't it; one minute I was praising and thanking Him, the next minute blaming Him and giving Him orders.

'Drive past the barrier and put your car in line ready for the ferry,' said the voice. I had no time nor desire to argue this time; I just drove onto the quay and, parking in line with the other vehicles waiting to board the next ferry, I stepped out of the car and queued at the ticket office; without enough money to buy a ticket. My turn came, I spoke to the cashier: 'One Mini camper and one person to Dover please,' I said handing over all my remaining notes.

You are such and such short, came the reply, my notes duly returned to me. Taking my purse, I turned it upside down letting all the loose change I had in different currencies fall onto the counter. 'This is all I have,' I said, holding my purse upside down for a moment to show there was nothing more to give. The cashier counted the loose change and, before I could catch up with what was happening, there before me lay a ticket for Dover, with even a bit of change left over; less than one pound. Moments later, I was back in my Mini and driving onto the ferry.

On the ferry deck I flopped into a vacant seat. What a journey! But how was it I was able to buy that ticket? I examined it closely; firstly, I had been charged one pound less than the man in the information bureau had quoted. Secondly, my loose change had been accepted, something I was told the cashier would not do. Little wonder the Lord told me to drive past the barrier and put my car in line ready to go. He knew I'd have just enough if I trusted and obeyed Him. I shuddered to think what would have happened had I been disobedient and filled that petrol tank the second time. With the remains of my loose change I bought a cup of tea and a sandwich.

We reached Dover in the pouring rain; I was back in England. I drove to Hythe in Kent, arriving around midnight, my heavenly companion still with me!

Chapter 11

Now what Lord? I had no idea what to do or where to go. On 5 October 1976, I drove to the YWAM centre in Sussex. I was simply trying to find out where I was meant to be and what I was supposed to do. Everything I possessed remained in my Mini as I had nowhere to put it. At the YWAM centre, I found exactly the same 'thing' that all the other young people had both at the Christian Centre in Salzburg, and at YWAM in Hurlach, Germany. It was clear they had received the gift of speaking in tongues. I remained with these people until 29 October, but I knew I was not yet in the place where the Lord wanted me. I witnessed wonderful things happening among those young people, and was able to question them on what I wanted to know. One incident stayed in my mind.

Back in England in 1976

One evening I went into a room to find a healing taking place. A lady sat people in a hard straight-backed chair, took hold of their ankles and measured if both legs were the same length. She then prayed for the shorter leg to grow, and I was told that legs grew! I've always had an open mind about this kind of healing; I neither believed, nor disbelieved. I could accept healing if it took place, but I could also accept it if it didn't take place.

As long as I can remember, when walking in the rain or on wet pavements, water had splashed up the back of my left leg. This always annoyed me. I had tried walking differently but it made no difference. So now it was my turn to sit on the hard straight-backed chair. Sitting bolt upright, the lady grasped my ankles and the length of both legs was examined. Yes, one was very slightly shorter than the other. Prayer was then made for the shorter leg to grow. I sat motionless while the lady told me she could see my leg growing. I felt nothing. When it had grown, the lady asked for the growth to stop, then she let go of my legs both of which now touched the ground. Getting up from the chair, I yelled in surprise at feeling unbalanced in the hip on my left side. I lurched forward unable to adjust immediately to the change and it took some hours before I was walking naturally again. Since then, I've never had any trouble walking in the rain; the back of my left leg has remained dry every time.

I now needed to earn some money and, as I had no home to go to, I applied to the same agency that had previously provided employment. At least I would have somewhere to live and could earn a living until I found out exactly where the Lord wanted me. The agency accepted me, and I was soon speeding off to my first lady client which was a short stay. The second client was far away in the West Country. It took me most of the day to drive there and on the way I was now became aware that my 'companion' who had accompanied me all the way from Salzburg was no longer beside me.

I always had a fear of going to other people's homes to be of service to them. You never knew what they were going to be like. I suppose the same went for them but this was the first of three very bad experiences.

The couple were elderly, as most of them were, but the wife appeared to resent me from the start. No matter how I tried, everything I did was wrong and, on reflection, I should have left the day after arriving.

There was a problem with the shopping; she disliked so many people in so many shops that I was limited to where I could go. That meant traipsing all over town to the precious few shops she still liked. Added to that, I would only go to shops that issued receipts to prove the price of my purchases as some clients I had known wanted to work out the cost of their shopping to the last farthing. While with this elderly couple, I enjoyed walking back to the house instead of taking the bus but for some reason this made the wife angry. Even the way I hung out the washing made her angry. I endured the job as best I could but was deeply unhappy. The wife barely spoke to me, and refused to make any kind of conversation except to give orders.

The situation came to a head when I inadvertently left my Bible on my bedside table instead of putting it under my pillow. Now there appeared to be open hatred; I could barely breathe without being criticised and, as a result, a crushing fear came over me. I didn't even feel safe in the bedroom I slept in. This went on for another two weeks until an incident that compelled me to leave.

On this particular day, I was being supervised over a twin-tub washing machine; as if a hawk was hovering over me ready to seize me as its prey. I was expected to take the washing from one side of the machine to the spinning side without a drop of water landing between the two tubs. Of course, it was impossible to prevent it and the old lady hovered with a cloth in her hand wiping every drip as it fell. She became very angry. With washing spun, I hung it out to dry in the garden but that was done all wrong too. By now I was too miserable to care. But back in the kitchen, I was ordered to wipe the inside of the washing machine. One of the drums was removed, electrical elements were laid bare and I was given a cloth supposedly to wipe them. But in a flash I was warned within; 'has the electricity been turned off?' In the state of mind I was in, I could have easily overlooked this rather important point.

I cast my eyes up to see the washing machine plug securely in its electrical socket and the switch turned on. The old lady read my mind. She moved quickly to turn off the switch. I made doubly sure it was off by ripping the plug from the socket quite convinced about what she had hoped to do to me. I refused to stay in that house any longer and after a call to the agency I left the next day.

For my next post I was given a frightening self-opinionated bully of a man who ordered me about and expected me to be at his beck and call every day until about 11 pm. He liked to be thought of as grand with all his valuable possessions and, on the other side of his conceit, he sneered at the books I read and the time I spent knitting in the evenings. Driving his car with him beside me was a nightmare, raking up leaves in the garden had to be done exactly his way. If I didn't carry out his commands, he sulked for hours like a spoilt child. I carried on as if nothing had happened but just how I survived three weeks there I don't know. I could have walked out earlier but what would the agency have thought? However, I did make a report after I'd left.

Leaving that terrible post, I was only to find a third. Mrs Thomas had been burgled and was afraid of being left alone. Her house had once been sumptuous; it stood in its own vast grounds, either a smallholding or farm of some kind. Soon after my arrival, one of the men who lived in a farm cottage picked me up to take Mrs Thomas shopping and quietly informed me she was an alcoholic. I'd never met an alcoholic before so didn't know what to expect. On our return from the shops, I took just what I needed from my Mini to go into the house, fortunately leaving most of my belongings where they were.

Only part of the house was in use, many rooms had furniture stacked in them and covered with sheets. But I could see it was beautiful furniture and it didn't take much imagination to see what the house used to look like.

Now a line of washing hung across the kitchen, dripping over a central table where meals were eaten. I found the whole atmosphere very frightening; I couldn't place it but it permeated everywhere and took hold of me with a real fear. Mrs Thomas was clearly drunk and reeked of alcohol but it was something more than that, something I could not describe.

I soon discovered a black cat that kept rubbing itself against my legs. I adore cats but this cat I wanted to kick outside. It unnerved me. Trying to be friendly, I picked it up, gave it milk but it filled me with the creeps and I couldn't bear it touching me. When I went to bed, I was too frightened to sleep restfully and was glad when daylight came. Among the first jobs was to take breakfast to Mrs Thomas in her bedroom. She reeked of alcohol, her speech was slurred and I found it difficult to understand what she was saying.

Because of the burglary, every window had locks which only opened with special keys. Nothing was opened during the day. At night, the burglar alarm was set and the thought of being locked in greatly added to my fear and claustrophobia.

As the morning went by, I was trying to clean the kitchen and I became more and more terrified of being in the house. The cat never stopped rubbing against me. Mrs Thomas was now incoherent, so unsteady on her feet she could hardly stand up. With her hovering around, I had just finished preparing a meal when something made me blurt out, 'I shall not be staying. You're drunk!'

Mrs Thomas responded in a tirade of anger and abuse. Never before had I seen such a sudden and complete personality change. She turned on me in a wild fury, ranting like a woman possessed. I expected to be physically struck.

Between chokes of tears and drips from the washing above us, I ate some of the meal and afterwards, when we had finished, cleared the plates from the table. Through Mrs Thomas's slurred speech, I understood enough to get her gist; apparently I was to stay to prove to her that I was a woman!

This didn't stop me though. I went to my room to pack the few things I'd brought in. Taking them downstairs, I found Mrs Thomas blocking my way and shouting. Surprisingly, I thought, she stepped aside to let me pass to the back door; but it was locked and I couldn't find the key anywhere. 'Open the door,' I said, 'I want to go out.' Mrs Thomas didn't move. I went back upstairs to the room I'd slept in but there was no way I could get out of the windows as they were locked. Downstairs again I went, taking the last of my belongings with me and leaving them with the others beside the back door.

Now she ordered me to go with her into her drawing-room to have a talk. I followed her; there seemed nothing else I could do. Inside the drawing-room, she stood by the telephone and I told her to phone the agency and repeat to them her rantings to me. Well, if she didn't then I would; I reached over and grabbed the phone, thrusting the receiver at her. 'Now tell the agency all you've accused me of,' I said.

A look of fear came over her and she backed away from me. 'You're a mess,' she shouted at me. What she meant I didn't know.

'Yes, I know,' I replied.

In an instant she completely changed again and, coming over to me, smothered my face in kisses. Taking me in her arms, she stroked my cheeks. I thought she had gone insane.

'Does the agency know?'

'Yes!'

'Does your family know?'

'Yes!'

'Oh, you poor darling!' she said.

I saw this as my way of escape. 'Surely you don't want anyone like me in your beautiful home. Why don't you unlock the door and get rid of me?'

'Yes,' she agreed. The back door was unlocked and, picking up my belongings, I walked to freedom. Outside, I saw the man who had told me about Mrs Thomas the previous day; I called him to come over. He was there in a flash while Mrs Thomas was asking me if she could do anything to help. Yes; I asked her to pay me what she owed me and thereupon, in the next instant, she was raving like a mad woman again. The man led her inside the house to quieten her down and I took the opportunity to check upstairs for the last time that I hadn't left anything behind.

With my Mini packed and shedding copious tears, the man invited me back to his cottage to rest a while. His wife and some friends who were staying with the couple wouldn't hear of my driving off that night so, as all the beds were occupied, I was offered a mattress on the living-room floor to sleep on. Apparently, they had waited up the previous evening until midnight in case I needed help. Mrs Thomas had caused a lot of trouble with the staff, hitting one at sometime, I was told. They also told me that none of their dogs would go into the house. They would go only as far as the front door, but never a step further.

That night I fell asleep on the mattress in front of a log fire that threw long leaping shadows onto the walls. I knew I had to find other work and a place to live. The next day I headed back to Hythe in Kent.

I stayed some weeks with Mummy; she must have relented a bit from her previous hard line. Also I stayed with my sister and brother-in-law (Barbara and Ralph) who lived a couple of hundred yards away.

The first job I took was at Portex, a company in Hythe that manufactured medical products. At least it was a start, and brought in funds that would be needed if I found a flat. I now searched in earnest for somewhere to live. One day, as I was walking along Seabrook Road, I saw a lady sweeping her front path. Just as I passed her, the inner voice said, 'speak to that person regarding somewhere to live.' Turning back, I introduced myself to her, asking if she knew where I could find some rooms or a flat to live in. Her face lit up in delight and surprise.

'Yes,' she said, 'we have a flat upstairs that is just about to become vacant, but we've never had a woman before, always a man. I'll ask my husband.' I moved in on 31 January 1977.

The next thing was regular worship at St Leonard's church. On some of my visits to Hythe, as far back as 1943, I attended services at this beautiful church, so it wasn't completely new to me. Now the time had come to go on the electoral roll, and share the joys of worshipping the Lord there every Sunday for many years to come.

My faithful Mini was still getting me around, still no leaking radiator, but she was showing her age and there was a lot of rust. Also, the year's insurance had almost expired so, despite the precious memories of my journey across Europe in her, I let her go. Apparently, a local garage had heard I wanted to sell her and two men came to see me; one said it was worth nothing, the other offered me £5. Silly isn't it, but when the young man drove her away, I felt a part of me had gone with her.

I didn't last four months at Portex. The noise and boredom of the repetitious production work contributed to my leaving. But it started me off again financially to pay the rent and for the necessities I now needed for my flat. The next job I took was in the sewing room at a school, a job I enjoyed and it left me the energy to pick up some housework jobs for elderly people in the afternoons.

Whit Sunday came on 14 May 1978 and began ordinarily. At St Leonard's Church, the beautiful red altar cloth contrasted with the ancient grey stone walls and pillars. The flowers, as always, were beautiful. There was something about the atmosphere of St Leonard's when I went there to worship that permeated my whole being. Not only was there a wonderful organ, always magnificently played, but just sitting in the pews lifted me into another dimension. I arrived for the usual 9.30 am Sung Eucharist but the day was to be rather significant. Remember I wrote about the part of the church service in my childhood when that 'something' happened every time we came to the words, 'we do not presume to come to this Thy table merciful Lord ...'? Well, here we were saying those words again, having lost count of the hundreds of times I must have repeated them since childhood.

The vicar was at the high altar, and the congregation praying aloud. My eyes were wide open, which they usually are when I'm praying. The beauty of the church absorbed me into it. Quite suddenly, I became aware of an ever intensifying spiritual atmosphere filling the place. It grew stronger and stronger, and I raised my eyes higher in wonder at what I was inwardly seeing. I expected the vicar to be carried up through the roof, or some manifestation to become apparent, so powerful had the atmosphere become. I shivered from head to foot, in great expectancy and thrill. At that moment, I realised I was speaking in tongues! So I had been given the gift. The vicar did not disappear through the roof, and the service continued as usual but, for me, it was another milestone in my spiritual life, taking me into the same realms of praise that I knew all those young people I had met previously had experienced.

I have to say a little about this wonderful gift as some years previously there had been a lot of controversy on the subject. This gift was received by multitudes of people, many of them young, but others who did not receive it felt neglected. Some, I fear, even felt a little inferior. For me, receiving this gift took me into another spiritual dimension. I could go beyond what human words could not express in prayer. Ever since 1953, I'd felt the Lord's 'inflow' of Himself but now there was, and still is, an 'outflow.' I feel as though one half of a circle has joined with the other half, which rotates in and out of me. Somehow, I'm 'joined up' in a new way, and feel complete in Him. This is the only way I can explain it.

Three months later, on 14 August 1978, I started working as a home help. For some time, I knew I had to look for other work. I had built up quite a lot of jobs of this nature so, in a sense, it was just a continuation of the same work.

What a great need there is for this type of work and, what's more, I believe you also have to be a certain 'type' of person to do it. The overall need lies much deeper than just shopping and cleaning. Most of the people I went to help just needed someone to talk to. They lived alone, and I brought to them relief. The ministry of the listening ear was all that was needed; working was not important but I always felt guilty if I didn't do some sort of job for them. By listening, you took on a great load whether you wanted it or not. Many clients had become so self-centred and miserable that no one came to visit them. They had the feeling that nobody cared which was really not true. Sadly, many had driven away their visitors by their incessant moaning and groaning. When I hear sad stories, especially at Christmas about the old and lonely, I often wonder where the fault lies; there are always two sides to a story and, if you only hear one side you cannot properly evaluate. But it's difficult to love the unlovely isn't it? Sadly, these are the very people who need our affection. They don't have to be old either. Many younger people can be in the same desperate need. I discovered that these people needed to get to know me first when a bond of trust was formed, and then they would let go and open up. Mostly, there was a cover to uncover. Some deep resentment, way back in the past; someone had hurt them; they had been mortally wounded and offended. 'I can never forgive them,' they would say. The wounds still lay wide open.

One old lady I went to enjoyed being housebound. She could have walked in and out of her house almost as easily as I did but she preferred to feel sorry for herself. Fortunately, she had many visitors although many complained to me that 'Mrs Smith could quite easily get up and get her own pension.' After I'd known this lady some time, I put this question to her, and she became angry and sulky. But it was the truth and she secretly knew it. We parted after a cold winter burst some water pipes in her house and caused a lot of damage, and she went to live somewhere else. Much later on, I heard she was up and about again involving herself in all the things she used to do.

Another person I visited was a similar case. Mrs Daly could hardly move her shoulders for pain, or so I was told. Everything I did was wrong. All the shopping was wrong. I'd ruined her stairs by knocking paint off them while cleaning. Two chair covers came out a different shade after I'd washed them; it was my fault as I'd used too much soap powder for one, and not enough for the other. One day on arrival, I hung my coat next to hers on an old hall stand, they were touching; she removed mine to another peg! I needed all the resolve I could muster to go and help her. In fact I dreaded going. But one day, I arrived through the unlocked front door and called my usual 'coo-ee.' There was no answer, so I walked to the back room half expecting to find her on the floor but to my amazement she was down the garden, hanging out her washing. When she finished, I saw her come up the path at a good pace but, immediately she saw me, she was bent over with a long face again. In fact, she almost fell onto the kitchen table; in utter exhaustion? Here was another prisoner in her own home. I confess that some people received a lot of straight talking from me. This one was no exception. When I asked her who locked her in and made her a prisoner, she became very bad tempered with me.

Some while later, as I was walking along the sea front where I had suggested Mrs Daly should go as there were seats to sit on, who did I see but this Mrs Daly all dressed up, sitting and enjoying the view and sunshine. 'Why hello Mrs Daly,' I said beaming at her.

'Good afternoon,' came a snooty, sneering reply. With a toss of her head, she looked the other way. Never mind, I thought, at least she's made the effort to get out of her self-imposed prison.

What inner needs we all have. But the causes do not always lie on the surface. I've found it's no good trying to cut the tops off; the roots need to be 'uprooted' as therein lays the root of the cause. Some roots go painfully deep down, and need major surgery to cut them out!

Some of the stories I heard I could hardly believe. The resentment that had been stored up inside for so long seemed incredible. 'But that was over 60 years ago,' I heard an 80 year-old say when unburdening herself to me. 'It's long past now,' she might add. But it wasn't, it was alive and doing well, fed and nurtured by a deliberate refusal to forget and forgive. Who of us has not loved to nurse a grievance at some time or other? Had the situation been different, we wouldn't be in the state we are in now, some of us argue. But would we be different?

I have come to the conclusion that the world is sick from the heaviness of unforgiveness, and in their hearts these people have rejected the only Person who can forgive us for not forgiving our neighbours which we are told to do.

The same old daily routine made life very quiet, dull and uneventful. There was the everlasting deep homesickness to return to the mountains and Austria. But I knew I was in the right groove on the Turntable and that it was a case of overcoming my own personal likes and dislikes which seemed to increase daily. But 'homesickness' is in the heart not in the head and that is not so easily dealt with.

It was now clear that Mummy was beginning to feel unsafe at night in her flat. What I'd dreaded now stood before me and, although my inner self was screaming at what I was doing, I offered to go and stay with her. It was for this situation, of course, that I had returned from Austria but I had hoped it would never materialise. Soon, though, all too soon I knew I'd be living with her and that happened sooner than I expected, as the owners of the house where I had my flat were splitting up and moving away. Now it was me who became full of resentment.

The excuse on my return from Austria for not living with Mummy was that the spare bedroom was not big enough for any permanent living; just as if I didn't know when I wasn't welcome. Now the room was big enough for me as long as I was needed. I was boiling mad and screamed at God: What more did He want from me? How much longer was I to give up everything? Was I never to enjoy a place of my own? Hadn't I given Him enough already? I'd sacrificed a career, turned my back on marriage, and never had a home I could call my own - what more? Deep in my heart, I knew there was only one person who could help me, and that was the One I was screaming at! I also knew perfectly well where the problem lay: in my total unacceptance of His will and purpose for me at that time. We've been through all this before haven't we, I thought.

Remember all those years ago when I had to apologise to the nurse who had put the rubbish in my clean wastepaper baskets? The problem was the same. Why should I after being treated the way I had been treated? Just because there was no-one else was she prepared to make use of me (although I'd willingly offered my services in the first place)? Here lay my deep resentment at the time. Actually, I was far better off at Mummy's flat than mine, and she was no trouble whatsoever. But I refused to think like that.

The readjustment was frightful. I'd lost the haven of my quiet kitchen at the back of my flat, and my peaceful evenings. But far, far worse, I'd lost my inner peace what with the noise of incessant traffic along Seabrook Road, plus the torture and horror of an over loud television for at least four hours every evening. If I crept into the bedroom to try and read, Mummy would come in wondering where I was. 'Oh, there you are, why don't you come into the sitting-room?' Never getting quiet evenings became mental torture.

One afternoon, as I peddled my bicycle up Sandgate Hill to Folkestone I was shouting loud and clear at God. No earthly person could have heard me as the incessant traffic deadened my voice. But the Lord heard me. In my heart, I heard Him say, 'I want all.' Just as if I didn't know. Up until now, He had had all, plus the groans and moans that periodically accompanied my 'all' but, for the time being, I preferred to be bitter and resentful. Very, slowly, He made it possible for me to accept His will and to surrender mine. It was a very slow process and what happened when I did this? My inner peace began to return!

From my diary - March 1980

'If someone had said to me, there could be a personal conversation with God, I would have doubted him or her. Yet, I am walking through one at this moment of my life, experiencing this communion.

'Inwardly I feel dead. I perform without feeling, going to my daily jobs without enthusiasm. My bounce has gone, and I feel dull and numb inside; even gardening, which I adore, has lost its joy.

'Now God is sharing His plans with me. He's showing me what He is doing and why He's doing it. There was much He tried to teach me, but I wouldn't accept it. Now, He is repeating the lesson again. He wants all the glory. I'm just His servant, washing His disciples' feet. Why then, was I expecting glory for myself? Why was I putting myself on a pedestal, thinking I should deserve this and that? Since when had I decided whose feet I would wash for Him? Had I not given Him full permission to be used as He liked? Why was I so hurt at doing this work He'd now asked me to do? Hadn't I offered in the first place? If I felt hurt, how did I think He felt at my angry rebellion against His will? Was I not so much better off living at my mother's? I paid no rent, bought no food, had every earthly comfort anyone could wish for. Why then was I so rebellious?

He now started to tell me I had an obligation to Him as His child! I was to share in the cross of His suffering. "Those who have been raised to life owe a compelling obligation to the Life Giver, which completely excludes selfishness!" He was not interested in my plans; neither did He have to ask if I would be willing to do this or that for Him. Had I not given myself freely? Had I not said, 'Thy will be done?'

Dimly, I began to see what the Lord was trying to teach me. I could not use any situation He put me into as an excuse for my attitude and behaviour. No matter what situation and testing He put me through, nothing could stop my becoming close to him. In fact, I was being tested to see if I would rise through it. Victory came after the battle and struggle, not without it. I grovelled on in the groove.

My quiet times became more precious. They became hallowed. His presence was felt as never before, and yet I felt so physically dead and weary to everything around me. This liberation of the spirit became clearer to me. Was this being 'dead to the world but alive to Christ?' Was this wonderful close communion giving me the mind of Christ, sharing His ways and plans with me? But does one have to be in the physical depths and sick at heart before that closeness becomes apparent? I was beginning to think so. I believed this was the only way we become broken bread and poured out wine. Those last few drops, still clinging to the vessel, that have to be shaken out with vigour before they are willing to drop away. We call from the depths, and we are dealt with in the depths, where the final dregs are dredged.

The battle raged on. It wasn't over yet. It was real, and the wounds were real. I seemed to go into a black tunnel, apparently losing all contact, or so it felt. Again I came to breaking point. I fought off tears, fearing that once I started I would never stop. One night, I couldn't stop them, and wept to the very depth of my soul. I felt I would crack up. I knew the signs. I'd been through this all so many times. 'Speak to me Lord! Where are You?' I cried. 'How much more can I take. When will it all end?' A great heaviness now descended upon me.

A few days later as I cycled to work, I found myself singing the line of a hymn, 'All for Jesus, all for Jesus...' It was like a stick of dynamite. It blew me inside out. My eyes were opened in a sudden flash of spiritual understanding. 'It's me I should be yelling at, not God!' 'I'm the one who has brought this about, by my selfishness, my total unacceptance of His will, my ungratefulness, my pride, my personal hurt.' I saw so clearly that my entire attitude was wrong. I couldn't blame anyone but myself and it came as a revelation. I rode home on wings of an eagle, not wheels of a bicycle. I sang along the bank of the Royal Military Canal, shouting my praises and halleluiah's.

Later that day back at Mummy's flat, the situation hadn't changed. It was exactly the same as when I'd left in the morning. But I had changed. I was at peace again.

On 13 December 1980, Mummy passed peacefully away. I hoped I'd learned the lessons that had to be repeated. I think I had.

Chapter 12

Sometime before Mummy died, I had a vague idea to visit my eldest sister (Monica) in New Zealand; but it was only an idea. I had also enquired about migrating to Australia but had been turned down owing to my age. I couldn't blame them. On the day Mummy died, I read in my daily reading: 'Perpetual Guidance ... wait for My guidance in every step.'

I was now free to go abroad again; back to Austria if I wanted to but I'd received no specific guidance in the matter. Knowing how easy it is to make a wrong move - and to slip out of the groove on the Turntable - I asked to be shown quite clearly where I was meant to go.

'Just name the country please Lord so there can be no mistake,' I asked.

The very next day the telephone rang. Someone with whom I had shared my thoughts on the subject asked if I'd like to have a chat with her about New Zealand; that was, if I was still thinking of going. Immediately I accepted New Zealand as the next country on my list but exactly where in New Zealand? I now made a request that was similar to the one I made years previously about where to go in Austria. 'Dear Lord, please pinpoint where I am to land in New Zealand.'

My sister Monica lived in Blenheim on New Zealand's South Island, so I wrote to her telling her of the possibility that I might be visiting; or, hopefully, staying. While waiting for a reply, I told those I worked for that I would be departing English shores in the not too distant future. Monica's reply soon came, advising that Blenheim was not quite the place for me; she thought that perhaps Wellington on the North Island would be a better place to make a start. Out came the atlas; so this was the first city to be pinpointed. I called a travel bureau to enquire about flights.

'Where do you want to land?' I was asked.

'I'm not quite sure,' I said.

'Oh, I expect it will be Wellington.'

'Ah yes!' So I accepted this as final; Wellington it would he. As a visitor, I only needed a visa for six months, plus proof that I could support myself financially; and a return ticket. Although I had all the confirmation I needed, I thought it would be good to receive further proof that Wellington should be my destination. It came about one week later while I was cycling in Hythe. I had been watching work on an extension of a building in Dental Street and, in doing so, almost fell off my bicycle. Recovering my composure, I looked up and saw a name board with the words 'Wellington Studio' carved on it. 'Lord! You really are good to give me yet more proof of where You want me to go!' I thought. Being confronted with the name for a third time seemed to reconfirm the message I already had. Although I had accepted it in faith, this third proof added weight to the guidance.

After a short wait my papers arrived. Now I could book my flight. I had no definite place to stay on arrival but there was always the YWCA. One lady I worked for gave me the address of friends she knew; they lived in Wellington! What that lady never knew was how significant was her slip of paper bearing the address. As she handed it to me, the inner voice said, 'these are the first people you are to contact on arrival.'

Getting organised included reducing my possessions to two suitcases again. What a hindrance earthly possessions are. The fact that I was leaving England in winter and arriving in New Zealand in mid-summer meant I had to take clothes for both seasons and be able to strip off on the way. I was also to take with me from Mummy's mantelpiece two fine china figurines that Monica had requested; family heirlooms that I called Jim and Joan.

Soon enough departure day, 11 February 1981, dawned, as did the beginning of another venture into the unknown, and yet another launching out in faith.

My first glimpse of New Zealand from the air revealed a landscape such as I'd never seen before, it looked like pumice stone and volcanic rock. The view over Queen Charlotte Sound was one of the loveliest I'd ever seen, the remaining parts of hills in the drowned valleys were wooded to the water's edge. As we bumped along the runway at Wellington International Airport, I wondered what my lot would be in this new country. Plunged into a hot summer from an English winter, my poor body was already suffering in the unaccustomed heat. At the airport, I quickly found a public phone and, at first unable to make it work, secured a bed at the YWCA and a taxi to take me there.

With all my travelling over the years, I was still overcome by the unfamiliar surroundings. Everything was so different; money, language (or rather accent), atmosphere, climate, food, way of life. In fact, as I had done so previously, I felt completely lost.

My taxi took me to the city centre and, after checking into the Y in Willis Street, I was looking forward to shaking off the long, tiring journey with a relaxing bath and then an answer to my immediate need; sleep.

However, it seemed a lot of construction was going on in the city centre. Huge trucks carrying excavated earth thundered along the street outside my room at the Y. The noise went on all night long; and the heat! My body felt like a blown-up balloon. My small bed, too, was uncomfortable, sagging badly in the centre. Even dragging the mattress off the bed to the floor didn't help. Sleep was impossible. People in the building came and went all night long, banging on doors outside my room. Then, in the early hours, there was more noise from outside as street cleaners and their trucks washed the streets. Despite my lack of sleep, I was up early, or so I thought. I knew breakfast was served from 7 am and waiting for the hour, I hung about in my room watching activity outside from my window but when eventually I went to the dining-room and was served a coldish cup of tea and a piece of bread and jam I discovered I hadn't put my watch on for the last part of the journey; it was already 9 am, not 7 am.

After breakfast, I contacted the address given to me by my friend in England. Again, I had difficulty using the public phone and it took me quite a while to find out why; numbers on the dial were placed differently to how they were in England. Number "1" occupied the place of England's zero. However, I had a lovely chat with my first contact Monica Willson and her husband, Geoff, and some days later I was invited not only to visit them but, after that, to make my base with them during my stay. No wonder I was 'told' to contact them.

Wellington seemed very hilly and windy. As I looked out of my room at the Y, it reminded me of San Francisco; the houses, dotted among the trees, had colourful roofs. Later, as I started my wanderings, I was thrilled to see trees and plants with exotic blooms for the first time. Thrill after thrill came as new plants, shrubs and trees presented themselves to me. I learnt within a day or two that the sun was exceptionally clear and what with the effect of of the wind too, my face, arms and legs became painfully burnt. With lashing of suntan lotion, it took three days for my face to tone down. Also, such were my wanderings that I developed blisters and sores on my feet and, maybe from the richness of the food, I had days of awful sickness and giddiness, possibly the price of finding the milk, butter and ice cream so delectable!

On 3 March, I began visiting some of the addresses I'd been given. The first took me to a Salvation Army lady named Rosie in Levin, 90 km north of Wellington. We arranged to meet after she had finished work at a thrift shop. Simple enough, but I caught the wrong coach with the wrong bus company and landed up at the wrong bus stop. But at least I was going in the right direction and, after discovering my mistake, the coach driver kindly delivered me to an alternative nearby bus stop. No-one was there when I arrived but eventually a flustered woman with a rather large voice appeared and in no time I was whisked away in a waiting taxi with me apologising for my stupidity and any inconvenience I'd caused. On arrival at Rosie's house, I was introduced to Honey, a big beautiful ginger pussy cat.

The next day I started work with the Sallies at a club for the over-60s. Before long, I was dashing around serving meals and pitching in to help wash vast piles of dirty plates and cutlery. For myself, I had difficulty in eating any quantity in such heat but I soon found out that Rosie had the constitution of a horse.

Among other club activities was an evening Bible study group where no-one could get away with just listening; questions needed to be answered too. Their collection day was coming up too within a few days and I was there to help. On the day, we were picked up at 8.30 am and taken to our allotted country area. Conforming to the climate, I was in my flimsiest of flimsies and stood beside Rosie's friend who was fully togged in Sally uniform, foundation garments, bonnet and all. As well as the heat, I was suffering from a bone-biting headache which I suspected was caused by two huge meals the previous day. Already at that early hour, I was sweating in my flimsies but with an SA sticker firmly adhering to my bosom I ventured forth. My SA companions were positively dripping.

As my collection box grew heavier, so did my feet and body. We were walking and the distance between houses seemed to get greater and greater. I was approaching exhaustion but I didn't dare complain. Rosie plus the lady who had brought us out in her car must have been in their 60s and 70s and they were surviving, even in their uniforms. Soon, however, I had to stop and was gratefully left to rest in long grass in the shade of a tree beside the lonely roadside while my two stoical companions drove off to a distant farm house.

Soon I began to recover but still had this awful headache. After a while, I began wandering down the deserted road while a horse in a nearby field followed me at a distance but never came close enough to say 'hello.' This struck me as strange. Were New Zealand horses a different breed? Surely not, so I made the first friendly move and, putting both hands over the rather high wire fence between us, I could just touch his body. Instantly, there was a kind of flash; I thought I'd been electrocuted. Current shot through me and into the poor horse. His flesh wrinkled and quivered in waves all across his back as he bolted away down the field. At the same time, both my arms shot up above my head. We - the horse and I - eyed each other in distant stony silence. Then I got the giggles. I sat down in the grass all of a tremble, thinking what an idiot I was not to have noticed the electric wire. Strange but then, to my amazement, I realised my headache had gone, and I felt wonderfully refreshed and recharged! From experience, I can readily recommend this form of treatment for headaches; preferably without foreknowledge! At 1.10 pm I was again joined by my sweltering companions. So the job was finished, at least for that day.

Sunday was spent worshipping with the Baptists in the morning and with the Sallies in the evening. On Monday evening we collected for another two hours in the town. On Tuesday, I was taken to the thrift shop to work. Behind the scenes, I helped staple coloured circles of paper on articles of clothing. Each colour denoted a price. I couldn't help thinking that if any elderly people felt they weren't needed or weren't useful any more, they only had to go to any Salvation Army centre and offer their services. So much voluntary work was available that no-one needed to feel unwanted.

A week or so later I had arranged to meet the next person on my list who lived not far away in Wanganui. I had written ahead saying I would be arriving on 11 March and would book a room at the local Y. After arriving by coach in the early afternoon, I went straight to the Y and inquired if there was a vacancy. 'How strange,' a girl at the information desk said, 'only yesterday someone came in and booked a room for an English lady. Could that be you?'

'Well no,' I replied, 'I've only just arrived.'

'Come back at 4 pm,' she said, 'the Matron will be here and she'll know the situation.' Leaving my luggage, I did a bit of sight-seeing and returned at 4 pm. Yes, I was the English lady referred to. I was ushered into a sun lounge where, on a central table was a basket with flowers, six cheese scones, two eggs, two tomatoes, two grapefruit, three apples and a letter. Mrs Blane wrote that she had visitors so was unable to put me up but, to make sure I had accommodation, she had booked a room for me. Indeed, I thought, my cup runneth over yet again. The sun lounge had French windows opening onto a garden. On the three nights I slept there, I took walks around the garden during the evening and what a beautiful experience it was. Although night time, it wasn't dark and oh, so warm. Breakfast was brought to me each morning on a tray from the Matron who invited me to watch television with her in the evenings. I was touched by the gracious hospitality.

I couldn't get used to the sun or moon, for that matter, moving across the earth on a different route as it were. The south was the cold side, while the north had the passage of the sun. It felt all back to front.

What free time Mrs Blane had, I spent with her at her home and was sorry not to have been able to stay longer. But at least I was able to write back to her sister in England to say I had visited her. Now it was time to return to Miramar, Wellington, and the Willsons who had opened the doors of their home to me. Their house was high up in the hills with views that were wonderful in every direction. There was the airport where I'd landed, part of Miramar itself, and a strip of water leading to Wellington Harbour from Queen Charlotte Sound. On another side, there was a hill of native bush. I loved watching the green ferries passing along the stretch of water, either on their way to Wellington, or to Picton on the South Island. The beaches were white, with bays sweeping into wooded cliffs and hills.

Everywhere you went, either to or from the house, was up or down. I forget how many steps led through a wooded area to Scorching Bay. I counted them umpteen times but always forgot the final number. Shrubs and trees bore colourful blossoms; it was a paradise to me being a gardener and feeling so at one with the beauty of nature and I could not help standing in awe at the vivid colours of flowers I'd never seen before. Crimson blooms on the eucalyptus trees, shrubs covered with pea-like flowers I never found a name for, great blue and white agapanthus plants lined the way down to the harbour, and blooms on the protea and callistemon (bottle brush) became even more magnificent when they were en mass.

We attended a Christian centre in Miramar on Sundays. It was always packed with youngsters and it was there that I really came to grips with the power of praise. At first I found it very emotional, recognising choruses from Austria, Germany, England - and now New Zealand. With an inner exuberance, I broke into singing, and nothing stood in the way to hinder the praise that issued forth from the depths of my being.

I began to understand the thoughts of the Psalmist when he wrote in Psalm 98 verse 4 onwards:

> 'Shout for joy to the Lord, all the earth, burst into jubilant song with music, make music to the Lord with the harp, with the harp

> and sound of singing, with trumpets and the blast of the ram's horn - shout for joy before the Lord, the King.
>
> 'Let the sea resound, and all that is in it, the world, and all who live in it.
>
> 'Let the rivers clap their hands, let the mountains sing together for joy;
>
> 'Let them sing before the Lord, for He comes to judge the earth. He will judge the world in righteousness and the peoples with equity.'

Jumping for joy for Jesus! No wonder the world may think us crazy when they see us. They wouldn't if they knew the Person we know. They don't think that jumping for joy at a football match is crazy. Give me Jesus any day; He's been my goal since I was 17 years old.

New Zealand, 1981

Once a fortnight, I helped at the fellowship session that provided a meal with a talk for any who came. It was a lot of work but very worthwhile. I got to know the people who came each time and there was a feeling of togetherness that I enjoyed very much. Looking back, I feel this centre helped channel and increase my growth in every way and have forever been thankful for what I heard, learned and shared from those wonderful gatherings that took place morning and evening each Sunday.

On 1 April 1981, I left Wellington by ferry for Picton on the South Island to visit Monica in Blenheim. Jim & Joan, the two fine china figurines from Mummy's mantelpiece, accompanied me. The day was perfect, the views idyllic; the little bays with their white sand, hills covered with native bush and yellow gorse, and the cleanest and purest sea I'd ever seen.

Soon the ferry was threading its way between the submerged hills in Queen Charlotte Sound; seagulls whirled and screamed in its wake. I watched from the open deck, the magic of the scenery, the clarity of the crystal clear green-blue waters below. This must have been like the world was before man polluted it, I thought. Picton, nestling between hills, slowly appeared in the distance. It reminded me of Austria with its picturesque lakes and villages at the water's edge, and stirred not a little homesickness. Briefly, I wondered if my sister had changed as it had been 12 years since I last saw her during her last visit to England.

The ferry arrived and suddenly I saw her close and, except for tinted hair, she hadn't really changed at all. After an emotional reunion, we drove off in her car to her home and, as we did so through the lovely scenery, I experienced a strange awakening in my heart. I was coming home again! It was wonderful to feel I belonged somewhere and Blenheim seemed like home, I could have settled there. Monica had a cute bungalow with a garden that grew all the flowers and shrubs that I loved. Oh how I longed for a place like that for myself.

After an enjoyable three weeks, I took the coach to Christchurch, about 350 km to the south, to see my niece Pamela (Blake née Moffat) and her husband, Peter. It was another glorious journey; up into the mountains then down to the coast road flanked by hills on the right and the clear blue-green sea on the left. Pamela and her family lived in a newly-built house in the suburbs of Christchurch and to explore the town and its environs, particularly the parks, I bought a bicycle and cycled everywhere. During my stay, I also booked a week's tour (9 to 16 May) but sadly lost an entire roll of film as it never rolled on. I therefore had only memories when I returned of the amazing variety of landscapes. One moment we could be passing through snow-clad mountain passes, then in a short while we'd be plunged into a tropical area of humid heat and soggy ferny forests. We passed through Arrowtown in all its autumn glory, and spent a night in Queenstown. The Remarkables, the mountain range on the south-eastern shore of Lake Wakatipu, already had snow on them and were attracting scores of brightly clad skiers. We crossed Lake Te Anau to visit some amazing underground glow-worm caves, and then on to the mighty Mount Cook (3,762 metres).

Back in Christchurch, I stayed until 15 June when I returned to Blenheim to celebrate my 53rd birthday (23 July) in mid-winter. Although the sun warmed each day to around 18C, it became quite cold after sunset. But even in the cool weather, there were always flowers to pick in my Monica's garden.

Soon it was spring again and lush green vegetation was once more everywhere. Monica and I worked hard in the garden interspersed with trips to various places, sometimes with friends. My final visit to Christchurch was in November (1981) to say goodbye to my niece Pamela and her husband; then also came my final stay in Blenheim, spending Christmas there. What an amazing experience it was, a mid-summer Christmas which we spent with some of Monica's friends who lived in Havelock, 40 km away.

For weeks beforehand, the shops had been filled with the same Christmas items that northern countries sell, Christmas cards with snow on them, paper chains, even a Father Christmas outside one store in the summer heat. Air conditioners were hard at work, ice creams were consumed as coolers; it all contrasted vividly with mid-winter Christmas in cold distant lands.

Christmas Day, 1981

Christmas Day was overcast and sultry. With Monica's friends, we set up a table in the outside shade surrounded by trees, flowers, bird song and distant hilltops bathed in mist, then sat down to eat a cold Christmas meal. When we had finished, three of us plus the family's lovely white goat, Sara, walked to a river not far away. We sat and chatted beside the rippling river which was as clear as glass while Sara wandered off to eat her own Christmas dinner of willow leaves. It certainly was a time to remember.

Most of the time in Blenheim, I'd gone to a Baptist church on Sundays, some walk from Monica's home. Then a new church, the Assemblies of God, opened much nearer and I went to visit. It was very modern looking, circular in shape with tiers of seats inside converging on a platform where a minister conducted services. Every Sunday the church was packed, accompanied by musicians playing different instruments; a thousand tongues to sing our Great Redeemer's Praise! The whole area for miles around must have heard us singing.

Sundays were for prophesais and healings and on one Sunday when I was there it was nothing new for me to hear someone speak in 'tongues.' Yet on this occasion, the service continued without interpretation. This interested me; there must be an interpretation, I thought to myself, as there always is. But no, this time there was none and, towards the end of the service, the pastor referred to the fact.

'I feel that these prophesy are for one person, or perhaps two at the most,' said the pastor, then he continued, 'travel, travel, travel ... You are anointed to this work ... You are to be a blessing and to be blessed ...'

I thought that the Lord might be speaking directly to me through the pastor. The words were verifying the past, and revealing the future. At that point, it was as though I was 'taken up' through the roof of the church; for a moment in time, I was no longer in time. Where I went I don't know but time stood still and I came back to find myself still standing in the same place but the pastor had stopped speaking. There was a pause, then he announced that if anyone present had clearly received a prophesy they may like to see him afterwards. The service was recorded each week, he explained, and a copy would be made available if required.

Seeing him later, I recalled what had happened. He asked me to wait two or three days, then phone his secretary; she would tell me how to get a copy of the prophesy. I waited a few days then phoned but was told something unusual had happened; the recording system had broken down and in fact none of the service had been recorded. My immediate reaction was great disappointment, I felt I'd been done out of something. But, on second thoughts, maybe never before had I asked for anything the Lord had said to me to be verified in writing. Why did I want it now? Deep down, I felt He'd played a mean trick on me! Why hadn't I been allowed to hear it all, especially as He knew in advance the recording system would break down? Later, the pastor rightly said, 'If the Lord wants you to remember what He said to you, He will bring it to your mind.'

So at last, bicycle sold, I left Blenheim for the last time. My year's permit was coming to an end and I was obliged to leave the country. The wrench of leaving New Zealand was as great as when I left Austria. I could have wept. It was only the second place where my heart said, 'you've come home.'

On 10 February 1982, I took wing to Sydney, Australia. Some years previously on a coach trip, I'd met a couple who had invited me to visit them if ever I was in the southern hemisphere. As in New Zealand, Australian authorities gave me a six month visa which could be extended to one year.

From Sydney, I flew on to Canberra where my friends, Arthur and Esther Freeman lived and once again I needed to re-adjust to different food and, oh my, even hotter temperatures. I was met on arrival and back at my friends' house was shown to my room and left to unpack but, as I went to a cupboard to hang up my coat, that inner voice said to me 'you won't be staying long.' As always, no time factor was given. How long is long, I thought; a week, a month? I had no idea. It turned out to be just over four months despite my plan for one year. Because of this inner information, I decided to leave most of my belongings in my two suitcases under the bed. I had no explanation for doing this; there was more than enough space to unpack my clothes, but maybe it was because I'd lived out of my suitcases for so long, or was it because I knew I wouldn't be staying long?

The heat was terrific, but the skies were blue and every day was wonderful continuous sunshine. I was surrounded by the most fabulous flowers, and streets were laid out with rows of many different kinds of trees. At the beach where I was taken, the sea was crystal clear. I was going to miss all this, and dreaded the day when I'd need to leave it all behind.

For the time being, though, I was faced with one deep problem, and I'm sure the Lord put me to the test as to what I would choose. I was urged to get a job; this was despite the words 'Employment Prohibited' clearly written on my visa. Half of me said it would be dishonest to work, the other half said how lovely it would be to earn back all the money I'd spent. What choice was I going to make? A verse from the Bible came quickly to mind: 'Give to Caesar what is Caesar's and to God what is God's.' Within me I knew an essential ingredient to spiritual well-being was honesty with God, and with man, and with oneself. But the temptation remained and with it an eagerness to pass off any sense of guilt as 'a little white lie.' But no lie is ever white. It's as black as sin, and sin places a partition between us and God, the partition breaking our relationship with Him.

The Oxford dictionary describes the word 'honest' as: 'Fair, righteous in speech and act, not lying, cheating or stealing, sincere, blameless.' Philippians 2: 14-15 says: 'Do everything without complaining or arguing, so that you may become blameless and pure, children of God without fault in a crooked and depraved generation, in which you shine like stars in the universe.'

Is this why the Lord insists on our being clean? That we may shine as lights wherever He chooses to place us? It was thus that I rendered to God what I believed was God's and to Caesar (the Australian authorities) what I believed was Caesar's. I chose not to seek employment.

I'm sure my decision was thought of by some as odd. 'After all, everybody does it,' someone said. 'So what, even the authorities know,' said another. But I was glad I made that choice, as very soon I was to witness another impossibility become possible. If I had taken a job, I would have missed out on another blessing that showed me again how nothing stands in the Lord's way when He wants to show His children that He is Lord!

Not having employment, I began sewing for the church that my friends attended. I sewed pieces of material from a charity shop into bags, or whatever. This kept me well occupied for part of the day. I also did a lot of walking and exploring, we had picnics and at the home of my friends' relatives I learnt to play snooker although not very well. But the abundance of experiences with nature was a constant fascination; being dive-bombed by a kookaburra, listening to the racket of cockatoos in the woods, stroking the silky fur of wallabies, watching kangaroos leaping as they ran, seeing emus for the first time. I was blessed to be in Canberra during the autumn, more magnificent than in New York. As the colours of autumn came out, so did my camera and over the weeks I built up a great library of slides, then in the dull winter days I'd have a slideshow which gave me a lift every time.

But then came a feeling I should leave. My hostess was not well which made me feel an intruder. Other friends invited me to join them on a trip around part of Australia. I knew that what money I had left would never cover the cost and a persistent inner voice kept saying 'no' to the trip. 'What shall I do Lord?' I asked Him. I began seeking clear guidance on what I was meant to do. The more I prayed, the more I knew I was not going on that trip and the more England seemed to be looming into view again. As the thought became stronger, I received very clear notice of what I had to do; go back to England and find a base.

It was a simple enough direction but, of course, there was a problem. My return air ticket to England started from Wellington, not Sydney. I was told by the airline that this meant buying another ticket and, emphatically, I could not use my existing ticket without first going back to Wellington. However, as with the trip I had been invited to join, I didn't have enough money to buy another ticket. I could not think of anything more absurd than flying back to New Zealand, then taking another three-hour flight back to Sydney before starting out for England.

I made a great matter of prayer about this. Clearly I'd been told to go back and find a base but why couldn't I leave from Sydney? Nothing clear was shown me, so a week later I visited the airline office again but was told the same thing. I was more than baffled; God was telling me to go back to England, I presumed from Sydney, but the airline was saying I couldn't. Was I wrong? Perhaps I had to go back to New Zealand first. Was this what God wanted? But the more I prayed, the more I was convinced the Lord was saying I should go back from Sydney.

I waited another week and, with new courage, set out to visit the airline office just once more in the knowledge that nothing could stop God's will; if I did my part, He would do the rest. Outside the office, in a car park, I did something I'd never done before. 'Lord,' I shouted, 'if You want me back in England as I know You do, I stand in Your authority against any hold up that is preventing me from returning to England from Sydney. Just clear the path, Lord, so that I can leave from here. I command in Your Name, all obstacles to be removed!'

I went limp. Just what had I said? What had I claimed? Never before had I taken hold of the promise that we have been given power to remove mountains; mountains of difficulties that hindered spiritual growth, and which are placed before us to see how we will vault over them. With jellied knees and quivering body, I went inside the airline office.

'Can I help you?' asked an assistant. Good, I thought, another member of staff this time.

'Well, I hope so,' I answered. I then proceeded to explain the problem for the third time, in the exact way I had done before. 'I have to return to England, but don't want to return to Wellington to start my flight. Can I start from Sydney instead?' Again I heard the deadly words, 'You'll have to buy another ticket as flying from Sydney isn't allowed on your existing ticket.' At that moment, the inner voice told me: 'book your flight.' So I booked my flight.

'I shall have to send for some money from England to pay for the new ticket as I haven't much left with me,' I told the lady. 'I just hope it will arrive in time.'

The woman looked at me, and then asked: 'Do you have your tickets with you?'

I knew immediately at that point that all the mountains of difficulty had collapsed before me. I handed her the tickets.

'A refund on these tickets should cover the cost,' she said. A calculation was quickly made; I would have to pay just 14 dollars extra. I handed over the money and a flight from Sydney to England was booked for 14

June 1982.

I left the office with normal knees and in utter amazement let out a yell of joy. The Lord had done it again. So the walls of Jericho had fallen down. The ingredients had been faith and obedience. Faith that I dared to believe the Lord could do the impossible, and obedience in obeying His command to 'book your flight.'

I didn't keep an account of the flight back to England. The route was about the same as the outward journey only the times were reversed. Night was day, and day was night; what I couldn't see on the outward journey because it was night, I was able to see this time. As we entered thick cloud on our final approach into London I remember thinking, 'Goodbye sun, I shan't be seeing you so often now.' I was again heading for Hythe, Kent, where my sister Barbara and brother-in-law, Ralph, had kindly offered to house me again until I was on my feet.

Back in England, I soon moved into a room in St John's in Hythe High Street, a place for 'old people.' To make ends meet, it was now back to everlasting housework and some gardening but what a joy to be back at St Leonard's Church. Now the search to find a 'base' began in earnest although I hadn't a clue what it was or where it would be.

Money in the bank was now greatly reduced. To rent a flat would cost more than I was earning. Buying a house didn't enter into it. Once again, I faced what seemed to be the impossible. Coming back from the vastness of Australia to Hythe, and a one room flat, nearly drove me insane. I found it impossible to stay in that one room for any length of time; it was as though walls in my head were falling inwards and I had to dash outside before things righted again. I walked and walked and walked; anything to avoid the claustrophobia that gripped me in enclosed places. The narrowness of Hythe High Street made me feel I was wearing blinkers. Everything now appeared so small and compact, like living in a box.

Four months after returning, on 21 October (1982), I went with two friends to a Lydia Prayer Conference at Herne Bay, and what an experience it was. It was there that I met Hilary Deedes from Aldington who was instrumental for my next move on the Turntable.

Already, I'd built up a lot of housework and gardening jobs, demanding all the energy I had but quite obviously the energy of youth was on the wane. Within a year, I could no longer manage two hours of housework in the morning as well as the afternoon.

All this time I had kept in contact with Hilary I'd met at Herne Bay and one day she contacted me to see if I would be interested in living in a mobile home in the countryside. It stood in the grounds of an elderly lady's bungalow; she just needed an eye kept on her, and to feel someone was close at hand. I was thrilled at the idea as it seemed just what was wanted so I arranged to meet the old lady and her son to discuss the matter. Just the thought of being in the country and living in a mobile home was a thrill in itself. The only problem I could see was that, as there were no buses, I would need transport to get me into Hythe each day so I could work. The interview went well, the old lady seemed charming, and I was ready to give her my care and attention.

The mobile home had been empty for years, and was infested with flies; alive, half alive, dead and disintegrated. In the ten months I was there, they hatched in their hundreds despite all my spraying. I never found out where they came from. Maybe from sheep in a field opposite; I wondered if they hatched outside and came in through the roof windows but, even if I kept the windows closed, they still came.

I moved out of St John's on 27 June 1983 and into the mobile home which I had by then cleaned up considerably. Beside the flies, I needed to clear out the belongings of the previous occupier, the old lady's sister who had lived there until she died. The few pieces of furniture I'd bought for my room at St John's fitted nicely and the old lady, herself, was in a nursing home after having a fall.

A local man sold me a Vauxhall Viva car but deep down I felt I shouldn't buy it. My plan was to put my bicycle (the one I'd bought in Austria which my sister had been looking after) in the back of the car, drive to Hythe where I'd park, then cycle to my jobs. All was set, so I thought. A lovely life in the country, no rent to pay in lieu of services rendered, a car and plenty of work. How good life was. I was indeed happy. In my spare time, I began to clear the overgrown around me in what had once been a well kept garden. At last I could walk out of my door and sit in the grounds, overlooking the fields with their sheep, and listen to the birds. Owls hooted at night in the darkness, the cuckoo called in the woods in spring. What more could I want? But I should have guessed! Since when had things gone smoothly like this?

The first problem to emerge was the car which refused to start in the mornings. Of course, it would start first try when I returned in the evenings but not in the mornings when I wanted to get to work. I was stranded; no public transport and I certainly couldn't cycle from Aldington to Hythe. Eventually, help came from a young, Peter Leonard, living just down the road who left home about 7.40 am. I was able to hitch a ride with him, putting my bike in the back of his van, and taking it as far as the County Members pub at Lympne where I'd lock it up and continue with Peter into Hythe. After work, I'd catch a bus back to the pub, picked up my bike and was home in half an hour.

The next problem came when Peter stopped going to Hythe and my car which by then I had nicknamed 'the beast' still wouldn't start. Fortunately, another neighbour came to my rescue; driving me to Folkestone each morning, and picking me up again around 4.30 pm. Meanwhile, 'the beast' sat outside the old lady's garage while I screamed and shouted at the harshness of my life. Would my life ever be anything but a damnable uphill struggle, I ranted. And with energy of youth waning, was I ever to have a place I could call my own? Where was this 'base' anyway, why couldn't I find it?

In retrospect, I like to think all this frustration had a purpose. Doors opened to witness for both neighbours who took me to work. I had told both of them what God had done for me in my life, and what He could be to them. Peter came to know the Lord personally, but I don't know about the other; I could have been just another link in a chain, and maybe there were many more links in his chain before it was completed. So, unknown to me at the time, the frustration I suffered was all part of God's grand plan on the Turntable. But what a frustration it was.

As for 'the beast,' eventually I found a wizard of a mechanic who discovered the fault and, with replacement part, the car leaped into action every morning.

Having surmounted my transport difficulty, the next awful problem was about to begin. The old lady returned from the nursing home but now where was the charm I'd seen at the interview? Apparently I was expected to be at her beck and call all day and every day. At first, I went to see her before I left for Hythe and asked if she wanted any shopping. She would delay me over trivialities and soon was giving me orders that I was to inform her at whatever time I returned. She shouted for me from her window, came to find out where I was, and what I was doing on the days I didn't go to work. Within a few weeks, life had become a living hell. She would sit at her window, watching for any movement from my front door, then shout for me to go and see her. If I dared walk across the grass instead of keeping to the path, I was put soundly in my place. Soon, to avoid her, I was returning home through a nearby copse and climbing over a fence of a nearby field. Weekends were the worst. I was constantly shouted for all day. I couldn't sit outside as she would wander down to find out what I was doing. If I didn't give her an account of my movements she became very angry and strutted away. I told her son that the conduct had to stop. Either she changed or I'd move.

I can't remember how the conversation started but one day I told the old lady about my life, and how I had once said, 'here am I Lord, send me.' She listened to all I had to tell her about the change He'd brought about in my life, the closing of doors to a career, and the life of wandering and witness in other countries and the jobs He had asked me to do. I could tell the words were sinking in and, within a short time, she had completely changed. She stopped her shouting, moans and demands and at this point I began to go into her bungalow more frequently. For a while, we had most interesting and pleasant times together. I wondered if she had had a personal experience and the Lord had spoken to her but, sadly, it only lasted about three weeks; then she was back to her old miserable demanding self.

But at least I resolved one of my problems, the Vauxhall; giving it away to a young family in Hythe. I was still in need of a car, though, and through an advertisement in a shop window in Hythe bought a Morris

Minor.

I was also still looking for a proper 'base' and one day was offered first refusal of a cottage in Hythe. Was this what I was looking for? I enquired if I could get a loan and I was told I could. But first I would need to get a job with more income.

'Now what Lord, is this, or is it not, the base I'm looking for?' A friend who looked over the cottage for me was not impressed. I was also in doubt, but I was longing to leave the old lady in Aldington. So I waited.

I was looking for a live-in job to tide me over between leaving Aldington and finding somewhere else to live and followed up on an advertisement by a convalescent home. I was accepted for the job but quickly regretting taking it. I can't ever remember experiencing such total physical exhaustion. I was on my feet for 10 hours a day, also my live-in room was unfurnished and I'd left all my private jobs to take the position. I was at the convalescent home only four days when I informed the housekeeper I wouldn't be staying.

What was I to do? 'Oh Lord, give me definite guidance concerning the cottage. I can't manage the job, I have nowhere to live, and I can't get a mortgage on the amount I'm earning. Just what am I expected to do?' The answer came quite quickly. 'Don't go into debt,' I was told and so I turned the cottage down. Picking up my private jobs again, I wondered what I was expected to do concerning this 'base.' I'd put all my belongings into my car to take them to the convalescent home, and now I had to take them out again and back to the mobile home. I did this undercover of darkness so as not to be disturbed. At least the Morris went well and I was thankful for one bright spot I could enjoy. The week at the convalescent home seemed to end my days in top gear. I never seemed to pick up to the same level of energy again. Something went out of me energy-wise that never returned. Now I knew I was growing older.

How I longed for a place where I could have peace, a place where I could have my own little garden, and could come and go as I pleased. I longed to live with the colours I liked around me, not forever having to put up with the distasteful and dull decors I had so often had to call home. I was tired of moving, moving, moving. 'Oh where is this base Lord? Why can't

I find it? How much longer can I go on like this? I'm so tired now.' But quite unknown to me I had passed this base once a week for ages.

One morning, as I was grousing mightily, He spoke to me through these wonderful words from my daily readings:

> 'Withdraw into the calm of communion with Me. Rest, rest in that calm and peace. Life knows no greater joy than you will find in converse and companionship with Me ... Do not fear. To fear is as foolish as if a small child with a small coin, but a rich father, fretted about how rent and rates should be paid, and what he or she would do about it. Is this work Mine or not? You need to trust Me for everything.'

Yes, I was beginning to carry all the load, little wonder I wasn't making it. How stupid, when the work wasn't mine but His! My load should have been only a small part, but I'd let it grow out of all proportion. I was anxious over everything, instead of being anxious for nothing.

Prospects of a base so far had been a house in Aldington but that came to nothing as it required borrowing money and I'd been told not to go into debt. Now a flat was offered to me but the rent was very high and it anyway had only a five year lease. No way; my 'base' had to be on a permanent basis. Then someone suggested I tried mobile home sites around the Hythe area, seeing that I liked living that kind of life.

For some years prior to my visit to New Zealand and Australia, I had attended a Bible study group in the Palmarsh, West Hythe. On the way there I had passed a pub called the Prince of Wales behind which was a park of neat, well-lit mobile homes. I had looked with longing at them and now, on returning to England, I was passing them again as I was back with the Bible study group.

One evening, for no reason, on my way to the study group I stopped and walked in to the park. An old lady was leaning out of her window in the first home I came to, so I asked her if she knew of a vacant plot. 'That's the man to see,' she said, pointing to the manager who was disappearing into the pub. I was just off after him when she called out again, 'the one behind me is up for sale!' Thanking her, I walked around to No 3 and immediately became excited; I knew it was the 'base' I'd been looking for. But how much was it? Did I have enough money to buy it? Would I never learn to trust the Lord completely?

I ran after the manager, keys were found to No 3, and the door unlocked. It was full of furniture, it reeked of cigar smoke which had stained everything inside but since when had I done much other than clean, clean, clean? At once I saw the potential and that evening phoned a solicitor handling the sale on behalf of his client. I told him I would buy it, would he kindly keep it for me. He promised I would have first refusal. Incredibly he added: 'You're just in time, it's being advertised tomorrow in the papers.'

Just what had made me go in to inquire? The next day might well have been too late. Well, anyone who has walked under the Lord's guidance will know the answer. The 'turn' and the 'time' on the Turntable were dovetailed again. It all fitted into place like a jig-saw. It couldn't have been any other way. Just why the Lord waits until the eleventh hour I don't know. Maybe that is the only way He can teach us reliance on Him. In a way, we are forced upon Him in utter desperation. What a lot of time He spends on our training, and how slow we are to trust Him completely.

Now I was able to inform the son of the old lady at Aldington that I would be moving out into my own mobile home; and so I did on 3 May 1984. By now I had completely fallen out with the old lady. I was so fed up with her moaning and continual interference that one morning I told her how I felt to her face. I was standing outside her front door at the time. She was livid and shouted at me that I should never set foot in her bungalow again and, with the force of a giant, slammed the door in my face.

My good neighbours, Peter and Evelyn Leonard, and friends in Aldington offered to help me move. As a precaution against being seen by the old lady, they backed their camper plus trailer across a field and we began to load up. Gone were the days of having only two suitcases and when the camper was full, we filled the trailer, topping it off with my rocking chair which I'd bought in Bournemouth in 1959. I was so happy that after almost 30 years, I finally had a place of my own; peace and security. No more hiding, no more escaping or running away. I could come and go as I pleased. The thought that no one could turn me out of this home, for which the deeds were drawn up, signed and sealed in the proper manner, was one of the most wonderful things that has ever happened to me.

At home and at peace: Shirley at the Prince of Wales caravan park in West Hythe, Kent, in 1988

Arriving at the Prince of Wales Park, we unloaded into my already full mobile home. Just where we put everything didn't seem to matter except I'd asked for a double bed to be removed to make room for my single bed and that evening a great big peace settled over me as I slid into beautiful sleep.

Over the days and weeks ahead, I had the task of cleaning my new home and getting rid of the previous owner's furniture. In fact it took me more than three months to get straight. Everything reeked of cigar smoke and had turned the furniture an awful nicotine yellow colour. With the massive cleaning job, very slowly the nicotine smell disappeared. I was also quick to cultivate the plot of ground around me. All the beautiful plants I'd loved since my childhood were planted and tended with loving care.

The year was 1984 and in July 1988 I would reach the ripe old age of 60. Wonderful, I thought, I can hardly wait. But retirement? If so from what? Certainly not from the Lord's work. Actually, in the kingdom, years are only measured from our 're-birth,' so that would make me 35 years old; lots of life in the old girl yet.

But what of time? I see the recording on my record has already passed the halfway mark. I trust the outstretched arm keeping me in the right place in the right groove won't have so much trouble with me in the future. Although my record hasn't played out yet, I'm aware that the circles are much smaller in circumference, and the central pivot holding it in place very much closer than it used to be. Also the speed has decreased. Not that the revolutions have ever been what I would describe as fast, but they are much slower now - far fewer revs per minute. From this viewpoint on the Turntable, I can look back and review the path I've walked so far. Where has the time gone? Why, it seems like yesterday I decided to step on to God's Turntable and let Him play His recording through my life.

Have I any regrets? The answer is definitely 'No!' The cost has been great, the sacrifice greater, but the gains have heavily outweighed any losses. I wouldn't want to repeat it all but, if it had to be, I wouldn't have it changed. I may never have a place in the Guinness Book of Records, but I am recorded somewhere in the Book of Life! When the record is played back to me - not videoed I hope as I've no desire to see it all again - the Arm that has held me in place will erase my heartbreaks, stumbles, falls and mistakes, and will present it 'faultless before the throne'. I hope I shall not be ashamed.

Epilogue

In July 2011, I shall be 83 years old. I see my record on the Turntable is slowly running down toward the end. Time is short. How many grooves? How many revolutions remain? How long do I have?

Looking back and having accepted His way, all the way without question, I'm now ready for the next installment. Where will that be I wonder; what has He in mind? Only time will tell.

To all who have managed to finish reading my story, I say a big 'Thank You.'

Finally I quote from the Book of Numbers, Chapter 6 (versus 24 to 26): 'the Lord bless you and keep you; the Lord makes his face to shine on you and be gracious to you; the Lord turn his face toward you and give you peace. Amen.'

Shirley
England, January 2011